AGATHA CHRISTIE

THE FINISHED PORTRAIT

AGATHA CHRISTIE

CHRISTIE

THE FINISHED PORTRAIT

DR ANDREW NORMAN

TEMPUS

Cover Illustration: Courtesy of EMPICS

First published 2006

Tempus Publishing Limited
The Mill, Brimscombe Port,
Stroud, Gloucestershire, GL5 2QG
www.tempus-publishing.com

British Library Cataloguing in Publication Data.
A catalogue record for this book is available from the British Library.

ISBN 0 7524 3990 1

Typesetting and origination by Tempus Publishing Limited
Printed in Great Britain

This Biography has been written in accordance with the definition of 'fair dealing... for
purposes of criticism or review' under copyright law.

Contents

Acknowledgements

I am grateful to the following for their help and encouragement:

British Medical Association, Tavistock Square, London; National Archives, Kew, Richmond, Surrey, UK; National Railway Museum, York.

British Library Newspapers, London; The *Daily Mail*; Harrogate Library and Information Centre, Harrogate, North Yorkshire, UK; The Old Swan Hotel, Harrogate, North Yorkshire (formerly the Harrogate Hydropathic); HarperCollins Publishers, London; The Random House Group.

Bob Hopkins; Sonya and Gabriel Chelvanayagam; Mary Bradley-Cox; Dr Julian Stern; Sophie Bradshaw.

And I am especially grateful to my dear wife Rachel, for her practical help and many insightful suggestions.

Introduction

Agatha Christie's novels and collections of short stories (translated into all the world's major languages) have recorded sales in excess of 2.3 billion copies, which is exceeded only by those of the Holy Bible. Her characters are equally famous throughout the world – and have achieved the status of super sleuths! But what of Agatha herself, their creator, the brains behind the legendary Hercule Poirot and Miss Marple? What is known about her?

David Suchet, the consummately brilliant portrayer of Hercule Poirot in numerous television dramas, who one might imagine would know more than most, is on record as saying, 'I don't know who she is'. Perhaps for this he may be forgiven, for throughout her life, Agatha remained a quiet, self-contained and retiring person who shunned publicity and rarely gave an interview. 'When you don't do a thing well, it is better not to attempt it, don't you think?'[1]

Discovering the real Agatha is a challenging, but by no means impossible task, and in order to do so it is necessary to employ such detective skills as might be worthy of her very own sleuths, Marple and Poirot. This is because, as with her detective novels, clues vital to the unravelling of the greatest mystery of them all, that of the author herself, are to be found in her writings, and in particular in the novels which she wrote under the pseudonym 'Mary Westmacott'.

By her own account, Agatha Christie had, in the main, a happy, secure, and fulfilled childhood, albeit punctuated by periods of loneliness. She was brought up in Torquay in the beautiful county of Devonshire, partook of that town's cultural activities, and made frequent excursions to Dartmoor – a place of mists and mystery, immortalized by Sir Arthur Conan Doyle in *The Hound of the Baskervilles* (which inspired her in her own writing). Later, she travelled to the Continent and became fluent in the French language and familiar with that country's customs. Her parents encouraged her in music and drama, and she also had access to her father's extensive library of classical novels. These experiences, and in particular the period she spent working in the dispensary of her local hospital during the First World War (where she familiarized herself with poisons), would stand her in good stead when it came to writing her famous detective stories featuring Miss Marple, Hercule Poirot, Parker Pyne, Tommy and Tuppence, and others. These would make her name known throughout the world.

Throughout her childhood, Agatha suffered from recurrent bad dreams, featuring a terrifying figure whom she called 'The Gunman' and whom she only managed to rid herself of in middle life. This torment is, perhaps, best reflected in her novel *Unfinished Portrait*, written under the pseudonym 'Mary Westmacott'. Ostensibly fiction, this, in reality, is the story of Agatha herself, in all its harrowing and lurid detail – hence the title of this volume *Agatha Christie: The Finished Portrait*.

Agatha had been brought up to have certain expectations: her principal professed aim in life being to achieve a happy marriage. However, having been launched into the world of the adult, her dreams would be shattered, and in such a brutal way as to temporarily unhinge her mind. As she herself admitted, her early life had been too sheltered. She had been too cocooned, and once the chrysalis had metamorphosed into a butterfly, the light of day proved too strong for it to bear.

An explanation for Agatha's bad dreams – which psychiatrists call 'night terrors' – is offered, and also for the means by which she finally overcame them. Also for her, seemingly, bizarre and inexplicable behaviour on the famous occasion of her disappearance for eleven days in December 1926, by which time life had become so stressful for her that she felt she could go on no longer. Why did she abandon her motor car, leaving behind inside it a fur coat, on what was a bitterly cold winter's night? Why did she adopt a false name, and claim that she came from Cape Town, South Africa? Why did she fail to recognize a photograph of her own daughter, or her husband when she was reunited with him? Was she telling deliberate lies, acting out an elaborate hoax in a cynical attempt to sell more books? Was this an attempt by her to punish her husband Archie, whom she knew was about to leave her? Or was there a deeper reason, whereby she became the victim of circumstances completely beyond her control? *Agatha Christie: The Finished Portrait* is an attempt to discover the truth.

The Miller Family

Agatha Mary Clarissa Miller (who became Agathá Christie) begins her autobiography by declaring that one of the most fortunate things that can happen to a person in their lifetime, is to have a happy childhood. Her childhood, she describes as 'very happy'. She loved her home and her garden; her nanny was 'wise and patient', and because her parents loved one another, this meant that they were successful, both in their marriage and in being parents.[1]

Agatha was born on 15 September 1890 at the Devonshire seaside resort of Torquay, an event which came about in the following way. Agatha's mother Clarissa ('Clara'), whose family came from Sussex, was born in Belfast in 1854. When Clara grew up she married Frederick Alvah Miller, an American who had moved to Manchester. (In fact, Frederick and Clara were related by marriage, Clara's Aunt Margaret being the second wife of Nathaniel Frary Miller, and Frederick being Nathaniel's son by his first wife Martha).[2] At the time of their marriage in April 1878, Frederick was aged thirty-two and Clara twenty-four.

The couple set up home in Torquay, and it was here, in 1879, that Agatha's sister Margaret – 'Madge' – was born. Finally, having returned to America, where in 1880 Agatha's brother Louis Montant – 'Monty' – was born, Frederick suggested to Clara that she set up home permanently in Torquay, where he would join her after concluding his business arrangements in New York. Using the money from a legacy, Clara promptly bought 'Ashfield', described as a sizeable mansion standing in extensive grounds which included 'an orchard, conservatories, a tennis court, and croquet lawn…'.[3] This is the house where Agatha was born, and around which her early life was centred, for as will be seen, her mother did not for some years consent to her attending school.

Of Agatha's love for her parents, there is no doubt. However, she describes her mother Clara as someone who had a habit of seeing the world as a drama, or even as a melodrama. Because of the creative nature of her imagination, she was never able to visualize places or events as being 'drab or ordinary'. She was also highly intuitive, which meant that she was often able to deduce the thoughts of others.[4]

Those who subscribe to there being a genetic basis for behaviour would argue that Agatha's own imaginativeness and creativity was inherited from her mother.

As for her father Frederick, she describes him as a lazy man of independent means; a collector of fine furniture and china, glass and paintings, who spent mornings and afternoons at his club, and, during the season, days at the cricket club – of which he was president – in Torquay. Nevertheless, Agatha acknowledged that Frederick had a loving nature, and was deeply concerned for his fellow men.[5] Frederick also possessed an extensive library which included comprehensive editions of the novels of the nineteenth century.[6] This facility would be of great benefit to Agatha in the years to come, in her own literary career.

Despite her father's undoubted inadequacies, Agatha had this to say about fathers in general. Everyone found the phrase 'father knows best' amusing, but nevertheless, it did epitomize the view that was prevalent in Victorian times. In other words, the father was 'the rock upon which the home was built.'[7]

Two other members of the family who would feature prominently in Agatha's life were Mary Ann Boehmer (*née* West), Agatha's maternal grandmother; she lived in Bayswater, London and was known as 'Grannie B'. Also, Mary Ann's sister Margaret Miller (*née* West), Agatha's maternal great aunt, who, after the death of her husband Nathaniel, moved from Cheshire to Ealing, Greater London. She was known as 'Auntie Grannie'.

Early Life

In Agatha's early years, home and family were paramount, and it is, therefore, not surprising that she became deeply attached to those who were assigned to look after her.

At Ashfield, Agatha's parents employed a nanny for Agatha. She was known as 'Nursie' and described as elderly and rheumatic. Agatha was devoted to Nursie, with whom she shared so much, for example, being allowed in the kitchen in order to help with the making of her own little bread loaves and plaited buns. When Nursie retired, Agatha described this as the 'first real sorrow of her life…'.[1] There was also a cook, Jane Rowe, who remained with the family for forty years, and several housemaids and a parlour-maid. In this seemingly idyllic world, however, all was not entirely sweetness and light. It was when she was about 5 years old, recalled Agatha, that her father first began to have money worries.

Her grandfather had invested his money in a series of trust funds, intended to provide income for his relatives after his death. However, the money that was due to come to Agatha's father did not materialize, either because of 'sheer inefficiency', or because one of the four trustees had managed to manipulate matters to their own advantage, which, Agatha did not know.[2] Agatha was at pains to stress, therefore, that although her father was an American, and all Americans were supposed to be rich, her family was not particularly well off. They had no carriage and horses; no butler or footman, and only three servants – which was a minimum in those days. However, poverty for the Miller family was only a matter of degree, because Agatha goes on to describe a typical meal served at Ashfield as including soup, boiled turbot or fillets of sole; followed by sorbet, saddle of mutton, lobster mayonnaise, pouding diplomatique and charlotte russe![3]

In order to economize, the Millers decided to let Ashfield, and spend the winter of 1895 in France where the cost of living was lower. Having crossed the Channel, Agatha described the excitement of going to bed in the train which would take them to Pau in the South of France, where they spent about six months. It was here that she went horse riding, and with the help of Marie Sijé, an assistant fitter whom they met in the dressmaker's shop, improved her French. Soon Agatha was able not only to converse fluently, but also to read books in the French language. When Clara asked Marie if she would care to accompany the family back to England, the latter was delighted. Then they left for Paris, to find the streets 'full of those new vehicles called *Automobiles*'.[4] They returned via Brittany and Guernsey.

These early experiences on the Continent would leave an indelible impression on Agatha; to the extent that she later chose to make her famous male detective a Belgian, whose charm was that he could view the British, and particularly the English with their traditions and eccentricities, from a Continental standpoint.

Although Agatha's elder siblings, sister Madge and brother Monty, had attended boarding school, their mother Clara became convinced that the best way to bring up girls was to give them as much freedom as possible, with good food and an abundance of fresh air. Their minds were not to be 'forced' in any way. Boys, of course, were an entirely different proposition. For them, education had to be along rigidly conventional lines.[5]

Clara also believed that children should not be permitted to read before they attained the age of 8 years, as this was better, not only for their eyesight, but also for their minds. Despite this, Agatha had learnt to read by the age of five, which opened up 'the world of story books' for her from then onwards.[6]

Nevertheless, Clara's action in keeping Agatha from school would be to her detriment, and would contribute to the serious psychological problems from which she suffered in her adult life, as will shortly become apparent.

A clear echo of Agatha's family home in Torquay – 'Ashfield', which was situated near the coast (and, incidentally, was poorly maintained through lack of funds), is to be found in a detective novel which she subsequently wrote entitled *Peril at End House*. This is a dwelling which a pretty young lady called Nick Buckley has inherited on the death of her brother. Nick refers to it by saying how much she loved it, despite the fact that it was 'tumble-down', and in an increasingly poor state of repair. Also, after an alleged attempt on her life, Nick describes a 'scrambly cliff path' leading down to the sea which she takes when she goes to bathe.[7]

Agatha's father Frederick died on 26 November 1901, when she was aged eleven. His health had gradually deteriorated, but despite this fact, no diagnosis had ever been made as to the exact nature of his illness.[8] (Agatha's mother Clara's perception of doctors as being, in the main, ignorant and incompetent is a theme which runs through Agatha's autobiography).

In September 1902, Agatha's sister Madge married James Watts, grandson of prosperous Manchester businessman Sir James Watts of Abney Hall. The couple set up home at nearby Cheadle Hall, and each Boxing Day the two families, traditionally, came together to attend the pantomime in Manchester.

When in 1903, Madge and James had a son, he was christened James, after his father and grandfather. James, or 'Jack' as he was known, with his blushing cheeks and golden hair, was an unending source of joy to her, said Agatha.[9] Meanwhile, back at home in Torquay, roller skating on the pier at the Assembly Rooms, or at the Bath Saloons (where at other times, the important dances were held), were favourite pastimes. However, at the Torquay Regatta, it was the accompanying fair, rather than the yacht racing, which attracted Agatha. She also describes garden parties where everyone was dressed up 'to the nines...'.[10]

It is recognized today, that a child develops his or her intellectual and inter-personal relationship skills more quickly when in the company of his peer group, say in nursery and junior schools and crèches, more than in isolation at home, and Agatha was undoubtedly deprived in this respect.

Also, it is sad to think of her as being lonely in her childhood, which by her own account she undoubtedly was, not only by being prevented from going to school, but also because her siblings Madge and Monty were a decade older than herself. She describes being particularly lonely after the retirement of Nursie, and later when her French governess Marie Sijé left and returned to France, having been with the family for three years. Equally detrimental to her well-being was the fact, that her upbringing in no way prepared her for the rough and tumble of adult life; a fact about which she would later complain bitterly.

On the other hand, had Agatha not been lonely, then perhaps she would have failed to develop that wonderful imagination with which she entertained herself, and which would one day stand her in such good stead when she embarked on her writing career.

A Love of Storytelling

That Agatha, from an early age, absolutely loved being read to can be deduced from her semi-autobiographical novel *Unfinished Portrait* (published in 1934, where the character of Agatha is represented by 'Celia'). Celia would ask her mother, Miriam, to tell her a story. She loved her mother's stories which were so different from those told by other people. To hear from them about Cinderella, Jack and the Beanstalk, and Red Riding Hood, was all very well; or from Nannie about Joseph and his brothers, or Moses in the bulrushes; but Mummy's stories were something quite special!

Part of the joy of listening to them was that one never knew what they were going to be about. The subject could be mice, children, princesses…. The problem was that she told her stories only once, and if you asked her to tell them a second time, she made the excuse that she could not remember. Then, with serious fact, but bright and shining eyes, she would gaze across the table, as she waited for inspiration to come to her. Suddenly, she would emerge from her trance-like state and proceed to tell a new story. It was to be called *The Curious Candle*. At this, Celia would draw in her breath with eager anticipation. Soon, she would not only be positively intrigued, but quite spellbound!

The inference is obvious. This, in reality, is Agatha speaking about her mother Clara, who had no need to refer to a book because she carried all her stories in her head. Again, it is difficult to escape the conclusion that Agatha inherited the same gift, for when she came to write her detective novels, she could juggle as many as eight or more characters in her mind, all interacting with each other, and everyone with motive and opportunity to commit the crime.

Agatha particularly enjoyed stories from the Old Testament and said that attending her local parish church of Tor Mohun was one of the highlights of her week.[1] Having learned to read at an early age, she was also able to enjoy the collections of fairy and animal stories given to her by Margaret Miller – 'Auntie Grannie'. She read these over and over again, and co-opted Marie her governess to re-enact various fairy stories with her at performances staged after dinner, in front of her parents Clara and Frederick.[2] In fact, drama was to play a large part in Agatha's upbringing, and she described visits to the local theatre in Torquay as one of the great joys of her life.[3] Auntie Grannie also fired the imagination of the young Agatha, by requesting her to recite juicy details of real life murder cases to her from the newspaper; this being a preoccupation of the Victorian and Edwardian press.[4]

Madge, her elder sister, was also instrumental in feeding Agatha's imaginative young mind, and it was she who told her her first Sherlock Holmes story. This was entitled *The Levenworth Case*. After that, she pestered her for more, and confessed to enjoying all of them – Madge being a splendid storyteller.[5] Among the great quantity of books which Agatha worked through were the novels of GA Henty, Stanley Weyman, and also the entire collection of Jules Verne in their original French. (Agatha's first lessons in French had been given to her by her sister Madge on the latter's return from finishing school in Paris. Agatha was only five at the time). Later she progressed in her reading to Charles Dickens, Sir Walter Scott, William Thackeray and Alexandre Dumas, authors of books which her mother enjoyed reading to her, just as she enjoyed being read to. An added bonus was that American novelist Henry James, and also English writer and poet Rudyard Kipling, were among those people who called at the house during Agatha's young days.[6]

Agatha read voraciously, and absorbed the stories told to her by members of her family as blotting paper absorbs ink. However, it was the works of Sir Arthur Conan Doyle, read to her by Madge, and the current criminal trials, which she in turn read to Auntie Grannie at the latter's request, which appear to have had the greatest impact on Agatha as a future writer.

A Creative Imagination

Time and again in her autobiography, Agatha alludes to the fact that it was her childhood loneliness which was the catalyst which led her to use her imagination to invent imaginary playmates and dramas. Nursie (her elderly nurse) was involved in the games which she enjoyed as a child, even though she was not always a participant in them. In fact, all the games were make-believe. From as early as she could remember, the imaginary companions that featured in these games were ones that she chose herself. She then goes on to describe 'The Kittens' whose names were 'Clover' and 'Blackie', and whose mother's name was 'Mrs Benson'. Later, there was 'Mrs Green' who had a hundred children: the important ones being 'Poodle', 'Squirrel' and 'Tree'. To supplement these imaginary creations were Nursie's repertoire of six stories, all of which revolved around the various children of the families by whom she had previously been employed. Agatha said Nursie, to her, was the epitomy of a 'rock of stability' in her life.[1] So here was Nursie, in company with Agatha's mother, sister, and grandparents, adding to the child's memory bank of stories.

By the time she was aged five, Agatha had created more imaginary characters, including 'Dickie' (based on Goldie the canary) and 'Dicksmistress' (based on herself). On her fifth birthday, she was given a dog, a four-month old Yorkshire terrier puppy which she named 'Toby'. The event, she said, gave her such unimaginable joy, that it left her practically speechless. Toby, as the character 'Lord Toby', was now given the special privilege of being admitted into what Agatha described as her 'new secret saga'.[2] She and Toby would now sit together under the dining room table, there to have imaginary adventures in equally imaginary locations such as underground cellars and such like.³ Dogs would play an important part in Agatha's life, and one in particular, not Toby but 'Peter', would be a source of comfort to her in the troubled times ahead.

Meanwhile, even inanimate objects could be transformed. For example, it was her hoop, said Agatha, which gave her most pleasure in childhood. It could represent to her such objects as a horse, a sea monster, or a railway train. She imagined herself to be alternately engine driver, guard, or passenger on three railways which were of her own invention.⁴ It was the hoop which solved Agatha's problem of being at a loss for a playmate when Nursie retired. She now retreated into her own little world with her hoop as her playmate.⁵ Other toys included a rocking horse, a dolls' house and a painted horse and cart – driven by pedals – all of which, also, doubtless featured in her make-believe adventures. When Agatha grew up and married, and had a daughter of her own, she could not understand why the child did not enjoy such simple pleasures as she had done in her own childhood.

Agatha's mother decided, finally, that her daughter, now in her early teens, should have a little 'schooling' at a school for girls in Torquay run by a Miss Guyer. A year later she was sent to school and then finishing school in Paris: the latter run by a Miss Dryden. Agatha described the two winters and one summer that she spent in Paris as amongst the happiest days she had ever known. At long last, she could enjoy the company of people her own age.

When Agatha returned home from school, however, the same problems of having nobody to play with persisted. She therefore invented yet more imaginary playmates, as there were no next-door neighbours who had children of her age. She also invented an imaginary school, sketching the characters of the girls and their different social stations, and describing their adventures and the games which they played together.

The Allure of Danger

In her autobiography, Agatha Christie gives her first hint that she actually enjoys being frightened. (And of course later, when she came to write her detective stories, she capitalized on the fact that the same is true of most other people, who like herself, enjoyed being frightened but only up to a point and within safe limits).

Agatha describes a terrifying game which she and her sister Madge played called 'The Elder Sister': a reference to an imaginary sibling senior to Madge and herself, who was mad and lived in a cave. Although Agatha, in her own words, would experience 'indescribable terror' when she and Madge played this game, nevertheless, she confessed that it was always played at her request. Similarly, the wood in the garden of her family home at Torquay was a place where her imagination could run wild.

This archetypal wood held, for Agatha, the prospect not only of venturing into the unknown and being frightened, but also of experiencing a 'secret delight…'. But why did she enjoy being frightened, or indeed terrified? Although there was no accounting for it, she did know that she was not alone, and that other children enjoyed stories to do with bears, wolves, and witches and so forth, just as she did. Could the reason be that there was something inside one which rebelled against a life that was 'too *safe*'? Did the fact that one was a human being imply that an element of danger was a necessity?[1]

While staying in France, at Pau in the Pyrenees, Agatha found two friends, Dorothy and Mary, and the three of them got up to a great deal of mischief. When they found themselves on a narrow parapet where they were obliged to walk virtually one behind the other, it simply did not occur to them that what they were doing might be dangerous. In fact, the parapet was situated on the fourth floor of the hotel at which they were staying. She could not remember whether they looked down from that great height towards the ground below, but even if they had done, she doubted if any of them would have experienced giddiness, let alone have fallen off. At the Cauterets, Agatha was invited to go horse riding with her father and sister Madge, despite the fact that her mother had certain misgivings.[2] Next morning, they mounted their horses – Agatha's animal seeming to her to be of immense proportions - and rode off, zig-zagging along up the 'precipitous paths' which she enjoyed enormously.[3]

As for real-life fear, this is something which she experienced when an angry man threatened to boil the five-year-old Agatha alive for trespassing on his property. This is an experience she most certainly did *not* enjoy. At this point she was really terrified, imagining herself immersed in a cauldron of boiling water above a fire.[4]

Agatha also experienced real fear following her father's death in 1901, when her mother suffered a number of heart attacks. She would wake at night, her heart pounding, certain that her mother had died. She acknowledged that she had always been endowed with a surfeit of imagination, and that this characteristic which, in her view, was fundamental to the craft of the novelist, had been useful to her in her profession. However, the down side was that it could make the life of a person of her disposition unpleasant in other ways.[5]

As Agatha grew up, the anticipation and thrill of danger remained with her. When friends of the family, the Ralston Patricks, took her for a ride in a motor car in the year 1909, she described it as one of the most 'adventurous days' of her life. Agatha described another car in which she was taken for a ride by its owner Mr Ankatell, as bright red, huge, powerful, and about 100 feet in length. This 'frightening, exciting monster' she found fascinating, with the gigantic pipes which protruded from it' bodywork.[6] In 1911, at a flying exhibition, and for the sum of £5, Agatha had a 5 minute flight: her first in an aeroplane, which she described as a 'wonderful' and ecstastic experience.[7]

In *At Bertram's Hotel*, Agatha's fictional character Lady Bess Sedgwick, appears to echo Agatha's own feelings when she declares that running into danger had virtually become a habit with her. In fact, it was more than that; more of an addiction. It was like taking a drug: heroin, for example, which addicts felt obliged to take from time to time in order that life should seem 'bright coloured and worth living' to them. She, however, had never taken drugs. In fact, she had never felt the need for them; danger being her drug.

Later, Bess says that one cannot help the way one is. She herself was unconventional, unconcerned with the law, and 'born to live dangerously'. Finally, having confessed to her crimes to Chief Inspector Davy, she also admits to him that he was absolutely correct when he said it was 'fun'. She had adored every minute of it: the 'scooping' of money from banks, railway trains, post offices, and what she sarcastically called 'security vans'! The planning of the operations he had also found fun. She would not have missed it for the world!

Here Agatha (whose factotums Jane Marple and Hercule Poirot almost invariably relish the joy of bringing criminals to justice) appears for once to see the other side, i.e. life from the criminal's point of view.

Crime writer Val McDermid discusses the part fear and danger play in Agatha's novels, and sums up the situation succinctly thus:

> One of the reasons we love any detective fiction is that it is safe to be scared in there, and we love to be scared safely. Adrenaline is a fantastic drug. It's legal. It's free, and we can turn it on almost at will. It's the fight or flight mechanism… [but finally] the detective will save us from what is bad and horrible out there.[8]

However, as far as murder – essential to the plot of so many of her books – is concerned, Agatha was easily able to separate fiction from reality. For her, and no doubt for the vast majority of her readers, capital crimes had to be kept firmly within the pages of the novel. As for real-life murder, she found the whole concept to be utterly abhorrent, as will be seen later.

Terrifying Dreams

To the outsider, Agatha as a child, led a seemingly idyllic existence. She lived in a beautiful place on the coast of the 'English Riviera'; loved both her parents as they loved her, and although lacking friends of her own age, was able to compensate for this by creating friends in her imagination. However, in every Garden of Eden there is a serpent, which in her case took the form of terrifying dreams.

For centuries, people have attempted to analyse dreams – the meaning of which can sometimes appear obvious, and at other times obscure. Agatha's dreams are instructive, in that they shed light on her mental state as a child. They indicate that, surprising as it may seem, she was a person who suffered from deep feelings of insecurity. As will be seen, this insecurity manifested itself most strongly when, in later life, a huge crisis occurred in which she had what would nowadays be termed a nervous breakdown.

In attempting to understand Agatha's bad dreams, it is first necessary to describe them. According to her, they centred around someone whom she called 'The Gunman'. She had given him this appellation, not because he carried a gun, nor because she was frightened of him shooting her. The gun, described as an antiquated kind of musket, was simply an appendage of someone who otherwise appeared to her as a Frenchman in pale blue uniform; his hair powdered and done up in a pigtail, and wearing a tricorn hat. No, it was the mere presence of the Frenchman that frightened her, together with the fact that he would appear during the course of a very ordinary dream, say when she was at a tea party, or walking with family or friends, or attending a festive event. Suddenly, she would be overcome with a feeling of uneasiness, knowing that there was

someone present '*who ought not to be there* '. This feeling quickly gave way
to 'a horrid feeling of fear', when she would suddenly see The Gunman,
either sitting at the tea table, walking along a beach, or joining in with
some party games. As soon as his pale blue eyes met hers, she would
awake screaming, 'The Gunman, The Gunman!'

There were, however, variations to the dream in that The Gunman,
instead of being a separate entity in himself, sometimes masqueraded as
another person. For example, Agatha would be sitting at the tea-table
when she would look across to one of her relations, or to a friend, and
realize that it was not her aunt, her brother, or her mother whom she was
looking at. Instead, as she looked at the familiar face with its characteristic,
pale-blue eyes, she would suddenly realize that it really was The Gunman.[1]
Agatha herself had no idea what the origin of these dreams was. Could
The Gunman have been derived from some story that she had read? No,
she had never read anything about anyone who remotely resembled him!

'Nightmares' or 'Night Terrors'?

Experts in the field of sleep disorders differentiate between night terrors
and nightmares:

> Night terrors, since they are disorders of arousal from the deepest sleep,
> occur typically, in the first part of the night – certainly the first half, and
> usually just a few hours after bedtime.

On the other hand, 'A nightmare… tends to occur towards the end of
the night – in the early morning hours.' In a night terror:

> Thrashing around, walking up and down in the crib, and seemingly terrified
> crying out are the results. He [or she] will not remember the night terror
> in the morning… Night terrors seem to occur in cycles. They may happen
> every night or so for several weeks, then disappear for months at a time.
> They are said to be outgrown by 8 years old in half the cases, but about a
> third of cases continue into adolescence.[2]

In her autobiography, Agatha gives the impression that her bad dreams
were most frequent when she was about the age of four,[3] and makes no

mention of them occurring in her teenage or adult years (even though certain traumatic events which occurred subsequently, were to remind her of them). From her description, it therefore appears, that what she suffered from as a child were night terrors (which an estimated five per cent of children experience), rather than nightmares; her symptoms appearing to fit well with the classical syndrome as described by psychiatrists.

Origin of 'The Gunman'

Perhaps the germ for the idea of The Gunman, the subject of Agatha's night terrors, was placed in her mind as a result of a game called 'The Elder Sister', which she used to play with her sister Madge. Just like The Gunman, this imaginary and terrifying Elder Sister was again *'someone who ought not to be there'*.

From Agatha's description, The Gunman was definitely male by gender – a Frenchman in uniform, carrying an antiquated kind of musket.[4] (Followers of the famous Austrian neurologist and founder of psychoanalysis Sigmund Freud, would undoubtedly support this view, seeing the musket as representing a masculine phallic symbol).

Is it, therefore, possible that Agatha feared that someone of male identity would take the place of her family and friends, and in particular her mother Clara, just as The Gunman did in her night terrors? This in turn begs the question, if Agatha suffered from a sense of insecurity, then why?

Attachment

Dr John Bowlby has made a study of the importance and significance of the attachment which occurs between the young child and its family, and in particular its parents. (He defines 'attachment' as being 'a reciprocal system of behaviours between an infant and a caregiver – generally the mother.') Says Bowlby:

> It seems likely that early attachment to one, or a few close relatives holds portent for a person's overall relational ability. Attachment predicts the ability to relate to many others; to establish trust, to form and retain friendships, and to engage in mutually satisfying emotional and physical relationships.[5]

Bowlby also advances the view:

> that excessive separation anxiety is usually caused by adverse family experi-
> ences, such as repeated threats of abandonment or rejections by parents, or
> to parents' or siblings' illnesses or deaths, for which the child feels responsi-
> ble.[6]

Separation Anxiety

No one is suggesting that Agatha was, in reality, separated from her parents, or indeed that either of them had any desire or intention to abandon
her. Quite the reverse, in fact. By not allowing Agatha to attend school,
Clara made her daughter Agatha dependent on the home and family, and
in particular, on herself and Nursie, far more than would normally have
been the case for a child. (Even when Agatha did eventually go to school,
it was only for two days a week).[7] When Clara and Frederick decided to
spend the winter on the Continent, they took Agatha with them. When
Clara sent Agatha to Paris to continue her schooling there, once again
she (Clara) accompanied her. It was the same when Clara went to Cairo
to convalesce after an illness. So why on earth should Agatha feel that her
parents might abandon her?

Possible Sources of this Anxiety

Of Agatha's love for her parents and her home there is no doubt, and
more than once she describes her own principal ambition as being to
reproduce this idyllic environment by achieving a happy marriage herself.
However, although Clara was there to comfort Agatha in times of trouble, as for instance when her canary 'Goldie' disappeared, or when she
was ill,[8] or when The Gunman appeared, and also to read her stories, one
gets the overwhelming impression that the child spent the major part of
her life alone – her older siblings, sister Madge and brother Monty, being
away at boarding school. Finding herself lonely and largely isolated from
other children, her survival mechanism was to invent a series of fictitious
characters: they would be her companions in the absence of real, live
ones. What little companionship she had, came either from her nanny, or

from her governess, and she was devastated, first when 'Nursie' retired, and later when Marie Sijé returned to France.

This imaginative and some might say over-sensitive child was aware that her own mother's childhood had been disrupted when the latter was sent away to be brought up by an aunt, who effectively adopted her whilst her three brothers remained at home. The bitter indignation which welled up inside her, the result of being made to feel surplus to requirements, adversely affected Clara's subsequent view of life, said Agatha. This unhappy event occurred as the result of an accident, in which Clara's father, Captain Frederick Boehmer, was thrown from his horse and sustained fatal injuries, whereupon her mother Mary Ann, was left at the age of twenty-seven with four children, and only her widow's pension to rely upon.[9] Did Agatha fear that a similar calamity might befall her own family? However, in no way could Frederick Boehmer be described in this context as a threatening figure, like The Gunman.

There were other factors which may have played a part in making Agatha feel insecure. Perhaps she wondered whether, like her two siblings, she would be sent to boarding school and was apprehensive on this account. Also, there was the fact that neither of her parents enjoyed good health. Were she to lose one, or even both of them, then this would be an even greater catastrophe.

Agatha's novel *Unfinished Portrait*, although purportedly fictional, is transparently semi-autobiographical, and it sheds further light on Agatha's (Celia in the story) dreams. It also indicates that not all of these dreams were of an unpleasant nature. Some were 'just funny and queer', about events which had actually happened, but which had become confused. Other dreams were 'specially nice' – about places with which she was familiar, and yet which in the dreams, seemed different. It was difficult for her to understand why having these dreams should be 'so thrilling', but none the less, it was.

Celia would dream that at the bottom of her garden, instead of the ugly red-brick house (presumably belonging to a neighbour), which was present in real life, there were 'dream fields'. Her greatest thrill was to dream of secret rooms within the confines of her house - access to them being through the pantry, or even from her father's study. She would then forget all about them until the next time, when she would dream of them again with an ecstatic feeling of déjà vu. Even though each time the rooms were quite different, that same 'curious secret joy' also returned whenever she rediscovered them. She would dream of a railway line which ran down to a lovely green valley with a shining stream, where primroses carpeted the banks and the woods.

These are what Sigmund Freud would have called 'wish-fulfilment' dreams – those which reflect the hopes and aspirations of the dreamer.

Who was The Gunman?

Did the threatening 'Gunman' of Agatha's dreams have his origin in a real-life person, or was he simply a representation, epitomizing all Agatha's fears and anxieties?

Paradoxically, a male figure whom Agatha may have regarded as a threat to the family was her own father Frederick, and for this reason: Agatha's family placed its reliance for the future on income to be provided by the investments from her grandfather Nathaniel Miller's will, but because these investments had been unwisely made, this income did not materialize.[1] Despite this setback, Frederick persistently refused to contemplate seeking any form of gainful employment, and the resultant financial insecurity caused his wife Clara much anxiety throughout Agatha's childhood. (Frederick's son Monty appears to have taken after his father somewhat, in this respect, as will shortly be seen).

This led Agatha herself to have grave forebodings about the future. The subject of 'ruin' featured often in the many books that she had read. This would cause the victim to threaten to blow out his brains, and force the heroine, who was now reduced to living in rags, to vacate the rich mansion that she occupied.[2] Believing passionately, on the one hand, that her father Frederick was 'the rock' upon which the home was established[3], and seeing the well-being of his household being jeopardized because of his inertia on the other, must have created a confusion in Agatha's mind which she would have found difficult to resolve.

Agatha's parents, and especially her father Frederick, caused her anxiety in another respect, because they both appeared not to take their Christian faith as seriously as she thought they should. This is borne out in *Unfinished Portrait*, where Celia (i.e. Agatha) is described as a 'serious' child, who gave

God much thought, and whose desire was to be 'good and holy'. However, one of Celia's greatest fears was that she was 'worldly', and she felt this particularly, when she was dressing up in her fine clothes, waiting to go downstairs to have dessert. In general, however, she was content in the knowledge that she was a member of the 'elect', one of those who would be '*saved*' (i.e. in the Christian sense of salvation). As for her family, they gave her 'horrible qualms', and she was tormented by the possibility that her mother Miriam – 'Mummy' – would not go to heaven.

The protocol in Celia's household was very strict. It was considered wicked, for example, to play croquet on a Sunday, and Celia would have 'died a willing martyr', rather than have picked up a croquet mallet on the 'Lord's Day', however much she might have delighted in playing the game on other days of the week. It was also considered wicked to play tunes on the pianoforte, unless, of course, they were hymn tunes. However, Celia noticed that both her parents chose to ignore these rules, neither appearing to have any scruples about playing croquet on a Sunday. In fact, her father went as far as to play song tunes on the pianoforte, which included such lewd phrases as, 'He called on Mrs C and took a cup of tea when Mr C had gone to town.' This was obviously an *un*holy song! Celia became so anxious that she sought the advice of Nannie, who now found herself in something of a quandary.

Nannie assured Celia that whereas she was sure that everything her father and mother did was absolutely correct, she was equally sure that it was important to keep the Sabbath Day holy. As for Celia's worries, she advised her to dismiss them, and to go on doing her duty. God had made a lovely world, and he wanted everyone to be happy. His own day was an exceptional one, where 'special treats' were permitted, just so long as no extra work was made for the servants. However, it was perfectly legitimate to enjoy oneself.

Much as Celia loved her mother, she did not permit the latter to influence her opinions. Nannie, however, was a different proposition: someone whose judgment she trusted. Something was true by virtue of the fact that Nannie knew it to be so. Celia therefore, took Nannie's advice and ceased to be concerned over her mother, who, incidentally, had a portrait of St Francis of Assisi hanging on her wall, and kept a small volume, entitled *The Imitation of Christ* beside her bed.

Celia was more anxious about her father, whose jokes about sacred matters, and in particular, one which he had recently told about a curate and a bishop, she did not find funny. In fact, she found it 'terrible'. Finally, she burst into tears, and felt compelled to voice her fears to her mother. Miriam reassured Celia that her father John, was a good and most religious man, who knelt down and said his prayers every night, just as children do. Celia, however, was not convinced, and pointed out to her mother that John made fun of clergymen, played games on Sundays, and sang unworldly songs. She feared that he would go to 'Hell Fire' (i.e. to hell). At this, her mother became angry, and demanded to know how Celia could possibly know anything about hell-fire. Hell is where people went if they were wicked, replied Celia. Who had been responsible for terrifying her with such matters, enquired her mother? To which Celia declared that she was not frightened. Instead, she was confident, that rather than going to hell-fire she would go to heaven because she would always be good. However, she was desperately anxious for Daddy to go to heaven also.

Alternatively, could The Gunman be a representation of Agatha's brother Monty, rather than of her father Frederick? After all, the former was a soldier, and would therefore have possessed a gun (although Agatha's Gunman dreams preceded Monty's joining the Army in 1899). As well as being a continual headache to his family, Monty was not a person whom Agatha appeared in any way to have liked. In fact, as will shortly be seen, there is evidence to suggest that she considered him to be temperamental and unkind. Also, Monty, who went to boarding school and later abroad, appeared only infrequently in Agatha's life, as did The Gunman. However, it seems unlikely that she saw him as a threat.

In her autobiography, Agatha's first mention of her Gunman dreams comes when she is aged four. Is it mere coincidence, that immediately prior to this, she describes the episode (already mentioned) when she leaves the immediate and safe confines of her home to go primrose-picking with Nursie? Suddenly, this idyllic scene of rural tranquillity is shattered. A huge and irritable man with ruddy complexion who, from the way he spoke, was probably a gamekeeper, appears from nowhere and accuses the pair of trespassing. What is far worse, he threatens Agatha with a horrific death – that of being boiled alive.

Agatha makes no mention of the man carrying a gun, and declares, that although she continued to have nightmares, this was not one of them. Nevertheless, it remains a possibility that in her subconscious mind, the gamekeeper became The Gunman of her night terrors.[5]

Were The Gunman to have his way…

Whatever the truth of the matter may be, one can imagine Agatha as a young child, retiring to bed, and perhaps playing a little game in her mind with her imaginary playmate before drifting off to sleep. She dreams that she is in a familiar setting, in the bosom of her family and friends, and all is well. Then, suddenly, The Gunman appears, threatening to supplant one or other of those whom she holds most dear, be they male or female, but in particular her mother Clara. She wakes up, screaming in terror.

When Agatha's father Frederick died, one of her worst fears was realized, as is indicated by her in *Unfinished Portrait*, where Frederick becomes 'John'. When John dies, Celia his daughter is dumbfounded. She finds herself in the garden, wandering about, trying to come to terms with the loss. For the moment, her world had collapsed. Although everything still looked the same – the ash tree, the path – it was somehow different. She was reminded of The Gun Man. Everything was quite normal until he appeared. She was now forced to accept the fact that '*Things could change – things could happen…*'. She wondered if her father was now in heaven, and if so, whether he was happy. Tears came into her eyes.

The subject of dreams has fascinated people from time immemorial, and their interpretation has taxed the brains of the world's greatest psychiatrists, psychologists and thinkers; not least the great Sigmund Freud himself. Even to those with a medical background, attempting to decipher a mass of psychiatrist's jargon, and make sense of, often, contradictory analyses by different persons of the same dream, is a daunting prospect – but nevertheless a fascinating one. Perhaps the most fruitful way forward is to study the works of those with long experience in the field of psychoanalysis, and then ask oneself what is the most likely explanation, bearing in mind that psychiatry remains, even today, more of an art than an exact science.

One of the most coherent explanations of dreams, in the context of the situation in which Agatha found herself, is to be found in the book *Dreaming and Thinking*, which is the work of analysts of the British Psycho-Analytical Society. Here, the contributions of Peter Fonagy, Gregorio Kohon, and J-B Pontalis are particularly relevant. The words of Peter Fonagy, in describing one of his patients, immediately strikes a chord, as his remarks could equally have applied to Agatha:

In her childhood, she was obsessed by her dolls' house dramas where it seemed that she enacted many of her feelings that were inaccessible to her through her natural process of reflection. At these times, her psychic reality was in pretend mode, completely isolated from what felt real and actual.[6]

Gregorio Kohon states that:

In the context of analytical treatment, we define dreams as the symbolic dramatic representations of past or present repressed wishes, trauma, and conflicts... In principle, dreams told by a patient in analysis can be considered more or less successful attempts by the patient to communicate to the analyst a situation of anxiety.[7]

According to J-B Pontalis:

My hypothesis is that every dream, as an object in analysis, refers to the maternal body... It is not the dream's contents, but the subject's 'use' of it that reveals his [or her] pathology. Dreaming is above all the attempt to maintain an impossible union with the mother, to preserve an undivided whole...[8]

This notion, (which can perhaps be extrapolated to include other family and friends, albeit to a lesser extent), is elaborated on further by Gregorio Kohon, whose 'primary object', in Agatha's case, would appear to be her mother Clara:

Separation from the primary object should promote, in normal circumstances, development and growth. As a consequence of the failure to separate [i.e. from her mother, for which, incidentally, Agatha cannot be blamed, as by being kept too long at home, she was unable to do so], one relevant feature of the patient's character is the inability to mourn. There is no real mourning for the object, only intense and vicious feelings at the possibility of its loss, which is at the core of his [or her] incapacity for psychic pain. The absence of the object is not tolerated; the absent object has become the bad, persecuting, malicious object, never to be trusted, present only to make the subject [i.e. Agatha] suffer. Since absence only confirms the failure of the subject's omnipotent control over the world around him, it is exclusively experienced in terms of a pending catastrophe.[9]

So here is Agatha, at a tender age and in the absence of friends to play with, living in the unreal world of dolls' house dramas, and as a consequence of being isolated, over-bonding with her mother from whom, in her subconscious mind, she was trying to break away. Yet, paradoxically, the great fear in her mind was of being separated from her mother (and to a lesser extent friends and family). This notion she cannot tolerate. It is seen as 'a pending catastrophe'. If it becomes a reality and she is abandoned, for whatever reason, she will now perceive her mother as 'a bad, persecuting, malicious object' – i.e. as The Gunman.

Of all the possibilities for the origin of The Gunman described above, this would seem to be the most likely. In other words, the sinister figure of Agatha's dreams represented not a man, but a woman.

The words of psychologist Calvin S Hall, who has made a study of dreams and their causation, would appear to lend weight to this notion: 'Strangers [such as The Gunman] represent the unknown, the ambiguous, and the uncertain.'[4] This said, it is difficult to escape the conclusion that Agatha, in her life, was a deeply insecure person, and that her night terrors were a reflection of this fact.

This fear of change, of losing her home, but more importantly of being separated from her loved ones, was a cardinal feature of Agatha's make up; a fact which was to have far-reaching consequences for her future well-being, as will be seen later when the idyllic world for which she had always longed, is shattered beyond recognition.

Writing, Music and Drama

Did Agatha always intend to be a writer? The answer is no, because in her youth, her main preoccupation was with music and drama. It was her mother Clara's wish that Agatha learn the pianoforte, which she did under the auspices of Fräulein Uder, a 'formidable little German woman'. She also learnt to dance at Torquay's Athenaeum Rooms, run by dancing mistress Miss Hickey, 'a wonderful, if alarming personality'.[1]

In her teens, Agatha played the mandolin in a small 'orchestra' which included the five daughters of the family of Dr Huxley – said to be the most sought after doctor in Torquay.[2] This little group, together with some other friends, were also to stage a performance of Gilbert and Sullivan's *The Yeomen of the Guard*. One of the highlights of Agatha's young life was going to the theatre in Exeter to see the famous veteran actor Sir Henry Irving playing in Alfred Lord Tennyson's tragic drama, *Becket*.

There are hints in Agatha's autobiography that she would dearly have liked to follow a career involving music or the stage. She shared her sister Madge's love for the operas of Richard Wagner, and dreamt that she herself might one day sing 'Isolde' (in Wagner's music-drama *Tristan and Isolde*) in a real-life opera. However, she was told that her voice was not strong enough to sing opera.[3]

After a year spent at the girls' school in Torquay, Agatha's mother transferred her to another in Paris, which she attended for about two months. She was now aged fifteen. Particular pleasures for her at this time included attending the opera, and learning dancing and deportment. She continued with her pianoforte lessons, this time under the auspices of an elderly lady called Madame Legrand, with whom she played duets. Sometimes, because of the zest with which her tutor played and her 'absorption' in the music, she failed to notice that Agatha had lost her place in playing the bass part. The result was, a 'hideous cacophony.'[4]

Agatha's mother now transferred her to a finishing school in Paris, run by a Miss Dryden. Here, she continued her education by attending the drama class and having singing lessons. Soon, she was able to sing many of Schubert's songs in German, and also arias from various famous Italian operas. During this period, May, the niece of her American godmother Mrs Sullivan, invited her to go to Italy to see Florence with its art and architecture.[5]

In 1910, Agatha returned home from Paris, by which time her mother was seriously ill. When the doctors who attended her made a variety of diagnoses, none of which were correct, Clara said, she therefore had no confidence in them. What she felt most strongly, however, was that it was vital to escape from the clutches of the medical profession. She then proposed to Agatha that they let the house and go to Egypt for the winter. (Some of the characters in Agatha's books were subsequently to echo her mother's thoughts by making the most scathing comments about the incompetence and inadequacy of the medical profession!)

For Agatha, the creative instinct to write was present from an early age, even though it did require a certain amount of prompting. After all, having read so avidly herself, and enjoyed being read to, it is hardly surprising that she herself, with encouragement from her mother and her sister, had little difficulty in putting pen to paper. The first story which she wrote as a child she described as a 'melodrama' concerning two noble ladies and a castle. She showed it to her sister, who proposed that they should perform it.

Agatha described her first attempts at poetry as being 'unbelievably awful'. However, she persevered, and duly appeared in print at the age of eleven, with a poem about the first trams (electrically powered omnibuses, running on rails) which came to Ealing. By her late teens, she had won several prizes and had some of her poems printed in *The Poetry Review*.[6] As for literature, Agatha was impressed by the works of English novelist May Sinclair; in particular *The Flaw in the Crystal*, probably because at this time, she herself was 'addicted to writing psychic stories…'. She declared, however, that her only ambition for the future was to have 'a happy marriage'.[7]

Agatha was lying in bed convalescing after an attack of influenza and feeling bored, when her mother suggested that she attempt to write a story. This she did, and it was called *The House of Beauty*. Several others followed, which she sent off to various magazines, but without success. All were typed by her on her sister Madge's Empire typewriter.

She then attempted to write a novel set in Cairo, and based on three characters which she had encountered in the dining room of the hotel there, where she and her mother had stayed. In that city, said Agatha, she attended five dances each week. She was then just 17 years old. At that time in her life, she admitted to having little interest in the 'wonders of antiquity', and for this reason she declined to accompany her mother on a journey up the Nile to Luxor and Karnak. However, the marvels of Egypt were to impress her mightily some twenty years later, as will be seen. Although she was, in her own words, having far too good a time to fall in love with anyone, Agatha revealed that she did receive at least two proposals of matrimony during this time![8]

The book which Agatha produced was entitled *Snow Upon the Desert*. When her mother Clara asked a neighbour, the novelist Eden Philpotts, to advise as to the next step, he put Agatha in contact with his own literary agent, Hughes Massie. Although Massie declined to accept this particular book, he encouraged Agatha by suggesting that she commence work on another.[9]

When Agatha said that she would like to try her hand at writing a detective story, her sister Madge's response was as follows. She had given it some thought, and decided that the project was too difficult a one for Agatha to undertake. This was seen not only as a challenge; it also triggered an obstinate streak in the younger sister. From that time onwards, Agatha was absolutely determined to write a detective story.[10] (Madge herself wrote a play, *The Claimant*, which was produced in 1924 in London's West End. One day, Agatha would follow in her footsteps by becoming a playwright herself).

Although Agatha's mother had denied her daughter a formal schooling until she was in her early teens, nevertheless it has to be said that it was Clara, along with her elder sister Madge, who appear to have been the main catalysts to Agatha becoming a writer.

Archie

In her youth Agatha had several suitors before she finally met her husband-to-be. They included naval sub-lieutenant Wilfred Pirie, with whom she developed a friendship, and to whom she even became unofficially engaged. However, the prospect of being married to Wilfred created in her, a soul-destroying sense of tedium. She felt that life with him would provide her with no excitement whatsoever. [1] Another suitor was Reggie Lucy, a major in the Gunners, who helped her to learn the game of golf. Having expressed his desire to marry Agatha, he and she became engaged, but Reggie made it clear that he was in no hurry to marry. In fact, he went away for a two-year period with his regiment. Meanwhile, Agatha looked forward to the day when she would be married. However, she was less enamoured about the role modern women had adopted for themselves, whilst at the same time being quite clear in her own mind as to what her role was to be when she finally did get married.

Agatha declared that the position of women, over the years, had not changed for the better, largely because women had 'behaved like mugs'. They had demanded to be allowed to do the same work as men, who in their turn had embraced the ideas all too readily. After all, why should they work to support a wife, when that wife was perfectly able to support herself? If this is what she wanted, then so be it! As far as Agatha was concerned, the sad thing was that women, having successfully portrayed themselves as the 'weaker sex', would now be roughly on the same level as those women of primitive tribes, who were obliged to labour all day in the fields. Agatha envied the women of Victorian times who, in her view, were in a much better position. In those days, women were seen as being frail, delicate, and in constant need of being 'protected and cherished'. In return for these favours, the woman accepted that the man was head of the household. When a woman married, she for her part, accepted the man's role in the world, and his way of life. These concepts appeared to Agatha to be sensible and the 'foundation of happiness'. She advised women who were not prepared to accept this state of affairs, not to marry![2] Agatha also believed that there was more to marriage than the couple simply being lovers. She took the old-fashioned view that *respect* was essential. The wife wished to feel that her husband was someone of integrity, someone on whom she could rely, and whose judgment she could have faith in. It was he who must be trustworthy, and reliable enough to make difficult decisions, as and when they needed to be made.[3]

Agatha first met her future husband Archie Christie, at a dance given by the Cliffords of Chudleigh, Devonshire, to which members of the local army garrison from Exeter were invited. It was 12 October 1912. She was aged twenty-two, and he twenty-three. From then on, the couple enjoyed going to dances and attending concerts together. Archie, an army officer, was currently awaiting admission to the newly created Royal Flying Corps, and would soon commence training on Salisbury Plain. He told Agatha, that as far as the Corps was concerned, if ever war was to break out again, then aeroplanes would be the first things that were required.[4] However, when Archie made Agatha a proposal of marriage, she declined, pointing out that she was already engaged (to Reggie Lucy). However, he persisted, and in the end, she relented.

Agatha described, in somewhat rueful terms, Archie's letters to her at that time. Instead of being romantic, as she had hoped, they were principally concerned with information about various aircraft, such as Farman biplanes and Avros. Nevertheless, to be involved with this new form of transportation – flying – was 'glamorous', she said. Archie was one of the first pilots to fly, and if she remembered correctly, his pilot's number was something just over the hundred: perhaps 105 or 106. She was enormously proud of him.[5] As for Agatha's mother Clara, she had reservations about Archie, whom she described as 'ruthless'. Sadly for Agatha, in this respect she proved to be correct.[6]

Agatha's own enjoyment of flying, however, would not be fulfilled by taking regular passenger flights (such as would soon become the norm across the world); this she described as 'prosaic'. No, as far as she was concerned, she had envisaged that to fly was to be like a soaring bird.

She longed to feel the thrill of 'swooping through the air'.[7] For Agatha, excitement, coupled with an element of danger, was meat and drink, and as already described, entirely in keeping with her character.

Brother Monty and the
First World War

Whereas her sister Madge (eleven years older) played a significant part in Agatha's early life, brother Monty (ten years older) was, more often than not, far from home. When the Boer War broke out in 1899, he volunteered for the Royal Welsh Regiment, and when the war ended in 1902, he obtained a commission in the East Surrey Regiment, leaving South Africa for India.

Agatha's novel hints at the relationship between herself and Monty – who is 'Cyril' in the story. Cyril is visiting home. He is clearly an adolescent as his voice is breaking: something which causes him embarrassment and makes him blush. Agatha describes Cyril as being 'gruff and uncomfortable', and prone to tears and tantrums. He is contemptuous when he sees her standing in front of the mirror, trying on some new clothes which she has purchased. This is the only thing 'a kid like you' is concerned with, he says; whereupon Celia bursts into tears, considering him to be most unkind.

Cyril joins the Army and goes to India, and later to Rhodesia. He now gradually disappeared from Celia's life. As for the real life Monty, he went to Africa, not to Rhodesia but to Uganda, where he became involved in a project to operate a fleet of cargo boats on that country's Lake Victoria, and to this end Agatha's sister Madge, invested the greater part of her capital in order that he could build a boat for himself. He responded by purchasing large quantities of 'luxurious silk pyjamas', which he presented to Madge, along with a bracelet set with sapphires, and other 'charming and expensive presents' – all, presumably, bought with her money! It was also noted that when he stayed with Madge and her husband James, Monty drank large quantities of whisky.[1]

In much the same way, 'Cyril' (Monty's equivalent in *Unfinished Portrait*) was also a source of anxiety to his mother 'Miriam' (Clara). Miriam, who is now elderly and frail, confides to her daughter Celia (Agatha), that she has been praying for some worthy gentleman to arrive on the scene; someone who would make Celia happy and provide her with a good home. She herself had but little money left, having had considerable outgoings on account of Cyril. There would, therefore, be little left for Celia when she had 'gone' – i.e. departed this life.

When the First World War broke out in 1914, Monty rejoined the Army – the King's African Rifles – and his boat was 'sold to the Government at a low price'. Monty was subsequently wounded in the arm. The wound became infected, and when he was discharged from the Army he returned to England, bringing his African servant Shebani with him. Having been successfully treated for his infection in London, Monty and his servant moved to Ashfield, the Millers' family home, and subsequently to a small bungalow on Dartmoor.

Early in 1914, Agatha passed her examination in First Aid and Home Nursing. This involved spending two mornings per week at the local hospital's Out-patients' Department in Torquay, and also spending a day with the District Nurse. She then joined the Voluntary Aid Detachment (VAD).

Following the outbreak of war on 4 August 1914, the first casualties began arriving at Torquay railway station, to be taken to an improvised 'hospital' – the converted Town Hall, where Agatha worked as a nursing auxiliary. With accommodation for over 200 patients, it was staffed by a matron, eight trained nurses, and VADs like Agatha, who enjoyed nursing and said, that had she not married, she would have 'trained as a real hospital nurse.'[1] On 5 August, her fiancé Archie, left for France with the British Expeditionary Force.

Agatha duly married Archie on Christmas Eve 1914. The couple then stayed at Torquay's Grand Hotel, and spent Christmas Day with Agatha's mother. On Boxing Day Agatha travelled with Archie to London and said goodbye to him as he left, once more, for France. She would not see him for another six months. In the summer of 1915, Agatha met Archie in London as he had three days of leave. It was not until October 1915 that the couple were to meet again; this time for a short break in Hampshire's New Forest. Three further periods of leave followed, but not until 1917.

During the war Archie displayed conspicuous bravery: being mentioned several times in dispatches and decorated with the CMG and the DSO. His days of active flying however, came to an end, owing to a sinus condition.

The Dispensary and the First Book

Late in 1915, Agatha commenced work at Torquay Hospital's dispensary. Here she studied for the Apothecaries Hall Examination, and was also given a certain amount of guidance from one of Torquay's leading commercial pharmacists. She now made, what in view of the course her future life was to take as a writer of detective fiction was concerned, a somewhat prophetic statement. It was only natural she said, that when one was new at this type of work, one was desperately anxious to avoid making any errors. Even though there was always another dispenser to check when a poison was added to a medicine, there could still be 'frightening moments', when a mistake could be made.[1] (The word 'poison' had different connotations in the early twentieth century to that which it has today. Then, pharmacists were governed by the Poisons and Pharmacy Act of 1908, where virtually all substances which would now be called 'medicines' were classed as 'poisons'). Agatha, subsequently, composed a poem entitled *In a Dispensary*, featuring poisons such as 'Monkshood Blue', 'Aconite', and 'Deadly Cyanide'.

One day, the pharmacist, whom Agatha referred to as 'Mr P', removed from his pocket 'a dark coloured lump', and asked her if she knew what it was. Then he told her it was curare: a substance which he found to be most interesting. When taken by mouth, it was entirely harmless. However, should it enter the bloodstream, it would first paralyse and then kill. He told her that it was used as an arrow poison. And why did he choose to keep it in his pocket? Because it made him feel powerful.[2]

The effect of this statement on the young Agatha, who was steeped in the adventures of Sherlock Holmes, and in the real-life murder trials which her Auntie Grannie requested her to read aloud from the daily newspapers, can be imagined. It was while she was working in the dispensary, said Agatha, that she first conceived the idea of writing a detective story. There being poisons all around her then, 'perhaps it was natural that death by poisoning should be the method I selected.'

In order to accomplish this, she decided that it was no use basing her ideas on actual people. A writer such as herself must create her own characters. She was able to put this into effect when she saw two women and a man riding on the tram with her, whom she thought would fit the bill admirably 'just as in the days of the Kittens [her imaginary childhood playmates]'. In other words, Agatha was now applying the same processes of character invention that she had used as a child.[3]

As for her detective, Agatha was determined that he should be quite different from others (such as Sir Arthur Conan Doyle's Sherlock Holmes). She, therefore, decided to make him a Belgian: there being a number of Belgian war refugees living in her local parish of Tor. A retired Chief of the Belgian Police Force, he would be tidy in his habits and very brainy[4] – the phrase the 'little grey cells of the mind' appealing to her in this regard. Finally, she settled on his name: Hercule Poirot.

One advantage of such a choice was, that having lived in France for a while and learnt the language, Agatha would have no difficulty in supplying Poirot, who spoke French with expressions: 'c'est entendu', 'eh bien', 'précisement' and so forth. Poirot, would also have as his colleague 'a kind of butt or stooge...'[5], namely, former soldier Captain Arthur Hastings, who had been invalided out of the army after being wounded in the First World War Battle of the Somme.

Having written the first draft of her book in longhand, and transcribed it, using the old typewriter that had once belonged to her sister Madge, she found that the intricacies of the plot were getting the better of her. Her mother then proposed that she go away for a holiday, in order to concentrate. The outcome was, that Agatha spent a fortnight at the Moorland Hotel at Hay Tor on Dartmoor, where she completed her book which she called *The Mysterious Affair at Styles*. However, the publisher to whom she sent the volume – Hodder & Stoughton – returned it. When she received a similar rejection from publisher Methuen, she then sent it to the Bodley Head, and promptly dismissed it from her mind. In the event, the Bodley Head kept Agatha's manuscript for almost two years before finally agreeing to publish, and then only after considerable changes were made.[6]

In her first published work, one might naturally have expected Agatha to write about subjects with which she was familiar, and this is precisely what she did. The setting for *The Mysterious Affair at Styles* is the fictitious Styles Court in Essex, home of the Cavendish family, and allegedly based on Abney Hall, family home of her brother-in-law James Watts, who in September 1902 had married Agatha's sister Madge.

Agatha described the real-life Abney Hall, where she and her family used to spend their Christmases, as being 'Victorian Gothic' with numerous 'rooms, passages, unexpected steps, back staircases, front staircases, alcoves, niches'; in fact all that a child could desire. Agatha also described a tunnel in the garden, which ran underneath the drive.[7] (This house would provide inspiration for several more of her stories, including *The Secret Chimneys, Hercule Poirot's Christmas, 4.50 from Paddington*, and *The Body in the Library*).

Although *The Mysterious Affair at Styles* was written on Dartmoor, there is nothing in the text to link it with that part of the world. However, there are several allusions to Agatha's own life. Styles Court is the home of the Cavendish family, with Mrs Mary Cavendish being described as full of life, dictatorial, with a propensity for 'charitable and social notoriety', and a predilection for performing opening ceremonies at fund-raising events in aid of charity, and for 'playing the Lady Bountiful'. When she hears of the plight of Cynthia Murdoch, daughter of an old school friend, who has been left orphaned and penniless, Mary takes her in and cares for her. Cynthia now finds work as a VAD in the Red Cross Hospital at Tadminster, 7 miles away. When Cynthia tells Hercule Poirot's confederate Captain Arthur Hastings, that she works in the Tadminster Hospital's dispensary, he enquires of her how many people she poisons. 'Oh, hundreds!' she replies.

As Hercule Poirot explains to Hastings, it is thanks to the good nature of Mrs Emily Inglethorp (Mrs Mary Cavendish's factotum, companion, and jack-of-all trades) that he was there. In fact, she had provided hospitality to no less than seven of his countrymen; all of whom were refugees from their native land. As Belgians, they would always look upon her with gratitude.

When Emily Inglethorp dies after a series of violent convulsions 'terrible to behold', the question is, who killed her, and with what was she poisoned? Although the story features Dr Bauerstein, a most able specialist from London, who was one of the greatest authorities on poisons at the time, it is Hercule Poirot who solves the mystery, by explaining how the introduction of bromide to a mixture containing strychnine will cause the strychnine to be precipitated. (In those days strychnine was given medicinally as a stimulant). This would mean that when the mixture was poured from the bottle, the last dose would contain the entire quantity of strychnine – i.e. it would prove to be a fatal dose.

It was undoubtedly as a result of her experiences at the dispensary that Agatha was able to familiarize herself with the properties of such substances as strychnine and bromide: facts which she assimilated and used in her first published novel.

As for Mr P, the pharmacist who kept curare in his pocket, Agatha described him as a potentially dangerous individual, despite his 'cherubic appearance'. The memory of him abided with her over the years, until the idea for writing her book *The Pale Horse* first came into her head, which was, she supposed, almost half a century later.

In *The Pale Horse*, which was published in 1961, the pharmacist Mr P, was reborn in the shape of Mr Zachariah Osborne who was 'respectably dapper', traditional in his ways, and one who liked to observe people in great detail.[8]

12

Poison!

One can imagine Agatha as dispenser in the hospital pharmacy, looking along the rows of medicine bottles, most of which were labelled 'POISON', as was the custom in those days, and being inspired to make death by poisoning central to the plot of many of her subsequent stories.

For example, in *One, Two Buckle My Shoe*, Mr Amberiotis is killed with an overdose of adrenaline and novocaine: normally used in combination by dentists as a local anaesthetic, but fatal when given as an overdose. In *The Chocolate Box*, Poirot discovers that the deceased Monsieur Paul Deroulard died as a result of eating a chocolate which contained several tablets of trinitrine inserted into it by the murderer. The effect of trinitrine is described thus: it was given to reduce high blood pressure, and to treat angina pectoris (paroxysms of intense pain in the chest, shoulder and arm, caused by a diseased heart). However, as the prescribing chemist says in the story, there are numerous substances other than poisons, which can prove fatal if taken as an overdose.

When in *4.50 from Paddington* Mr Luther Crackenthorpe's son Alfred dies after eating a curry containing arsenic, temporary housekeeper Lucy Eyelsbarrow suggests that the curry might disguise the taste of the poison. Whereupon, Inspector Craddock informs her that arsenic has no taste. When Alfred's brother Harold is also murdered, Inspector Craddock reveals that this was done by substituting tablets containing aconite for his normal tablets – aconite being a plant otherwise known as Monkshood, all parts of which are poisonous.

In *Triangle at Rhodes*, Valentine Chantry drinks a poisoned glass of pink gin, whereupon her lips turn blue, her hand goes to her heart, and she gasps as she fights for her breath. In this case, the poison used is stropanthin (derived from plants of the Stropanthus family), described as 'a heart poison'.

Perhaps the poison with the most bizarre effects of all is phosphorus, used by the murderer in *Dumb Witness* to kill his victim Miss Emily Arundell. For years, Miss Arundell had suffered with 'liver trouble', says Dr Donaldson, who points out the similarity in symptoms of phosphorus poisoning, and an attack of liver disease. In other words, by choosing phosphorus as his poison of choice, the murderer hopes to avoid suspicion. In the story, a feature of phosphorus poisoning is that prior to the person experiencing any other symptoms, his or her breath may become phosphorescent. In Miss Arundell's case this caused her breath to appear as 'a luminous haze'.

In *A Pocket Full of Rye*, Mr Rex Fortescue's house is called 'Yewtree Lodge', there being situated in its grounds a vast yew tree. When Mr Fortescue is murdered, Professor Bob Bernsdorff of St Jude's Hospital hazards a guess, that by a strange coincidence, the poison used to kill him is taxin (spelt 'taxine' in the story), an alkaloid obtained from the leaves or berries of the yew tree. Police Inspector Neele suspects that the taxin was added to Mr Fortescue's cup of coffee, in which case, the acrid flavour of the coffee would have disguised the taste of the taxin. In the same story, Inspector Neele tells Mrs Adele Fortescue some things which might surprise her. For example, in a case of digitalis intoxication with which he was involved, the poisoning, rather than being intentional, happened by accident. This was because in mistake for horseradish, foxglove leaves had been picked instead. The foxglove (Latin name *Digitalis Purpura*) contains digitalin, especially in its leaves: a substance which is used medicinally to strengthen the failing heart, but which, when given as an overdose, can cause death by excessively slowing the heart (a medical condition known as 'bradycardia').

In *The Moving Finger*, there is a discussion between Superintendent Nash and Doctor Owen Griffith over the death of lawyer's wife Mrs Symmington. When Nash ventures the opinion, that if one was contemplating suicide, it might be considered more sensible to overdose oneself with a soporific (sleep-inducing drug such as barbiturate), rather than to drink prussic acid, Doctor Griffith disagrees, in that, in his view, prussic acid was far more likely to 'do the trick'. With barbiturates, for example, provided that only a short time had elapsed, the victim could be restored to life again. However, in this case, he was absolutely certain that cyanide poisoning was the cause of death.

Not only was Agatha, through her work in the dispensary, familiar with the actions of a wide variety of drugs including poisons, she was also familiar with the signs and symptoms of various diseases, which again, she makes use of in her writing. For example, in *A Pocket Full of Rye*, Inspector Neele asks Percival Fortescue whether he suspected that his father Rex, may have been suffering from what was commonly known as GPI (General Paralysis of the Insane, the late result of a syphilitic infection), the symptoms of which were 'megalomania' and an irascibility, which finally ends in 'hopeless insanity'.

As everyone knows, Agatha went on, subsequently, to become a crime writer – the most successful one in history. But what would have happened had she decided to become a doctor instead? Surely, with her powers of observation, attention to detail, intuition and deduction, no patient would have been at risk from his or her complaint remaining undiagnosed!

13

Married Life with Archie

When Archie was posted to the Air Ministry in London, the couple set up home there in a rented flat. Agatha now commenced a study of book-keeping and shorthand, but confessed to being lonely. She missed the hospital, the friends whom she had made there, and the day to day routine. She also missed the surroundings of her home.[1] Finally, on 11 November 1918, the Armistice was signed and the First World War ended. Archie had now reached the rank of colonel at the young age of twenty-nine. He took some leave and the couple went to Torquay, where Agatha realized that she was pregnant. She rejoiced in the fact that in those days, the ante-natal clinics which subsequently came into existence, and where one was manhandled at regular intervals, had not yet been invented, because in her view, it was preferable to be without them.[2]

For Agatha, the achievement of a happy marriage was a top priority. Now, here she was, with the dashing, masterful and exciting Archie, the man she had selected from several suitors. She would create a happy and loving home, both for her husband and for the forthcoming child, who would be loved and cherished, just as her own parents had loved and cherished her. The odds appeared to be greatly in her favour, or were they?

On 5 August 1919, Agatha gave birth to a daughter Rosalind, to whom, according to her autobiography, she became absolutely devoted. One of her first actions was to redecorate the nursery, where the wallpaper would include 'an expensive frieze' purchased from 'Heal's store in Tottenham Court Road, and adorned with animals.[3] Rosalind had two toy teddy bears: Blue Teddy and Red Teddy; her favourite being Blue Teddy. He was her constant companion, said Agatha, who was required to tell stories about him every evening.[4]

A month previously, Agatha's cook and general maid Lucy had fortuitously reappeared on the scene, having been recently demobilized from the Women's Auxiliary Air Force – WAAF. Now Agatha employed a nanny for Rosalind – Jessie Swannell. When Lucy left to get married she was replaced by Rose. As for husband Archie, on his demobilization, he commenced work in the City.

Following publication of *The Mysterious Affair at Styles* (in the USA in 1920 and in England in 1921) the review which pleased Agatha the most was that which appeared in *The Pharmaceutical Journal*. This praised her detective story on the grounds, that its author clearly had a good understanding of poisons, and had not made the common mistake of referring to 'untraceable substances', as was often the case with other writers.[5] Nonetheless, even at this early stage of the marriage, there were signs that Agatha was not entirely happy.

When Agatha voiced to Archie her fears about the expense of keeping up Ashfield, the family home in Torquay, he said the best thing would be for her mother to sell it and go live elsewhere.[6] Agatha was horrified and refused point blank. In that case, said Archie, the only alternative was for her to write another book – which she duly did. She also supplemented her income by having her work serialized in *The Weekly Times*.

With Archie's increasing dedication to golf, Agatha found herself spending every weekend at the golf course at East Croydon, which was not to her liking. She missed the enjoyment of visiting new places, and taking long walks.[7] Nevertheless, her faith in Archie was unshaken, and even her mother Clara, despite her initial reservations, was beginning to come round to the idea that he might make an acceptable husband. This is revealed in *Unfinished Portrait*.

Miriam, who is in poor health, confides to her daughter Celia that she had been wrong about Celia's husband Dermot. When Celia had married him, Miriam felt that he was neither honest nor loyal, and that he was not be trusted. She fully expected that he would be unfaithful to Celia, who admitted that her husband was attractive to women, but assured her that golf balls were the only things that he was really interested in. Now, Miriam believed that she had been wrong, and that Dermot would look after Celia, even after her (Miriam's) death. She was also pleased to be told that Dermot was a homely person, and she genuinely believed that he loved their daughter Judy. But then, referring to Judy, she uttered words which would have cut Celia to the quick, even though the latter must, in her heart, have realized the truth of them: 'She is exactly like him. She's not like you. She's Dermot's child,' whereupon Celia acknowledged, albeit reluctantly, that this was something of which she was already aware.

Miriam confides to her daughter that at first, she regarded Dermot as someone who was 'cruel' and 'ruthless'. Now, she was anxious that he would be kind to Celia, who for her part was sure that he would be. After all, this had been the situation before Judy was born. Dermot was not the type to be verbally demonstrative, but deep down he was 'like a rock'. Miriam now admitted that in the early days she had been jealous, and also had, perhaps, failed to appreciate Dermot's good qualities. All she wanted now, was for her darling daughter to be happy. Celia assured her that she was.

As for Clara, Agatha's mother, who in a similar way had a change of heart about Archie, her first impressions of her daughter's husband-to-be would unfortunately prove to be all too correct.

14

More Ingredients for Stories

Torquay

In Agatha's novel *Dead Man's Folly*, where her home town of Torquay appears under its own name, a young lady from Holland who is visiting England for a two-week holiday, describes this well known beauty spot in glowing terms. Tomorrow, she proposes to cross the river to Plymouth, from where the 'discovery of the New World was made'. (This is a reference to the Pilgrim Fathers, who in 1620 sailed from Southampton, via Plymouth, to found the first colony in New England, at New Plymouth, Massachusetts).

In her novel *Peril at End House*, although Agatha speaks of the Cornish coast, there is little doubt that she is thinking of her home county of Devon: St Loo being Torquay, and the Majestic Hotel being based on the real life Imperial Hotel. The story begins by extolling the virtues of St Loo, which is described as being more attractive than any other town in the south of England. Not for nothing was it named the Queen of Watering Places. In fact, it reminded her strongly of the French Riviera, the coast of Cornwall being, in her view, equally as intriguing as that of the south coast of France.

Agatha then describes the Majestic Hotel as the biggest in St Loo. Situated on a headland overlooking the sea, its grounds included fine gardens which were adorned with palm trees. The sea was beautifully blue; the sky above cloudless, and the sun shone just as vigorously as it *should* shine in August, but in England frequently did not!

The Coast and Bathing

Agatha describes how, when the first trams came to Torquay, it was possible to catch one at the lower end of Burton Road, where her home Ashfield was situated, and be transported down to the harbour. From here, a walk of about 20 minutes brought one to Meadfoot, with its sea road and beach.[1] In Agatha's early years, sea bathing was strictly segregated: there being a bathing cove, albeit with a pebbly beach adjacent to the bath saloons, which was specially set aside for the ladies. In those days, in order to bathe it was necessary, in the interests of modesty, to enter a bathing machine - 'a gaily-painted striped affair' - and change into a bathing costume before being wheeled down into the water. For the gentlemen, there was a separate 'Bathing Cove' situated further along the coast. Finally, just after the beginning of the twentieth century, when Agatha was about thirteen, mixed bathing was permitted for the first time. Bathing being one of the joys of her life.[2]

One of Agatha's favourite local locations was the 28 acre Burgh Island, situated offshore from the resort of Bigbury-on-Sea on the south Devon coast. It was purchased in 1929 by millionaire Archibald Nettlefold, who built a luxurious art deco hotel there. The island is separated from the mainland by a sand-bar, across which a passenger-carrying 'sea tractor' can operate in up to 6 feet of water, in all but the roughest conditions. The island would feature in two of her novels: *Evil under the Sun*, where it was said to be isolated from the mainland at high-tide, and also in *And Then There Were None*.

Dartmoor

When as a child, Agatha found herself alone at Ashfield, her mother having been ordered abroad by the doctor for relaxation and a change of scene, she made friends with a family called Lucy, with whom she enjoyed expeditions to the moor (Dartmoor), having previously agreed to meet at Torre Station and take a certain train.[3]

In *The Sittaford Mystery*, Agatha reveals her love of Dartmoor when she describes vicariously, through the character of Emily Trefusis, an early-morning walk taken in that place. The lane ran steeply uphill to the open moor where it became a mere track, before disappearing altogether.

The morning was bright, chilly, and crisp, and the views were delightful. Emily climbed to the top of Sittaford Tor, which consisted of rocks piled up into bizarre shapes. (In fact, this effect must have been produced by a process of erosion). From here, the moorland appeared to stretch to infinity, unpunctuated by either dwellings or roads. In fact, the only other feature of interest were several large accumulations of granite boulders and rocks which she could see in the distance.

Agatha, writing from the heart about an area which she knows so well, goes on to portray a fictitious village called Sittaford, which included 'a smithy' (i.e. blacksmith's, this being the ideal terrain for a horse), and a post office-cum-sweet shop. Sittaford is situated, not down in the valley, as was customary for the majority of the villages and farms, but high up on the moor, and in the lee of Sittaford Beacon, the nearest town being Exhampton, which was 6 miles distant. There is also reference to a prisoner escaping from Princetown – where the notorious real-life Dartmoor prison is situated. At the time in question, there had been heavy snowfalls all over the country for several days, and here, on the edge of Dartmoor, it had accumulated to a depth of many feet. This, for the residents of the little village of Sittaford, was a very real concern because owing to the severity of the winter, they were now almost totally isolated.

A vital clue to the murder of Captain Joseph Trevelyan is given in the story when the Captain, and his friend Major John Burnaby, are described as great athletes who used to go to Switzerland together for the winter sports, and Trevelyan himself as a 'wonderful man on ice'. It finally transpires that the murderer, instead of travelling on foot to murder Captain Trevelyan, surreptitiously used skis, in order to save time and establish his alibi.

Both in her autobiography and in her detective stories, Agatha makes frequent mention of the author Sir Arthur Conan Doyle, and of his protégé Sherlock Holmes. Surely, in her perambulations on Dartmoor, Sir Arthur's *The Hound of the Baskervilles* would have been very much in her mind, for this is the place that Doyle himself had in his mind when he wrote the famous story.

Aeroplanes

With a husband who had served in the Royal Flying Corps, it is not surprising that Agatha should write stories relating to aircraft. For example, the story of *The Moving Finger* is told by Squadron Leader Gerry Burton, an airman who was injured after crashing his plane in a flying accident.

Death in the Clouds describes a journey on the airliner *Prometheus* from Le Bourget aerodrome, France, to Croydon, UK. As the aircraft flies over the Channel, the head of Madame Giselle, one of the passengers, 'lolled forward a little'. It might be assumed that she was sleeping, but this was not the case, for she was now capable of neither speech nor thought. In fact, Madame Giselle was dead. At first, it appears that she died of shock, having been stung by a wasp. Poirot, however, observant as ever, notices an unusual looking thorn with a discoloured tip embedded in her neck. She had, in fact, been killed by a poison-tipped dart.

Golf

Although Agatha was in no way as enthusiastic about golf as her husband Archie, nonetheless she was a proficient player, who even went so far as to win a handicap competition at the game.

In *Murder in the Mews*, Mrs Barbara Allen is found dead in her mews apartment (which she shares with a friend Miss Jane Plenderleith), with a pistol in her right hand, having been shot in the head. Once again, it is Poirot who solves the mystery by noticing from her golf clubs, that the dead woman was left-handed, and therefore, had she committed suicide, she would have held the gun in her left hand and not her right.

In *Why Didn't They Ask Evans?* Bobby Jones ('not the American-born master of the game…') is playing golf at a small seaside town on the Welsh coast, when he drives his ball over the edge of a cliff. In going to retrieve it, he discovers a man who is dying with a broken back whose last words to him are, '*Why didn't they ask Evans?*' Although the verdict on the dead man is 'death by misadventure', it transpires that he was pushed over the cliff deliberately. There are references to 'mashies' (lofted iron clubs) and 'niblicks' (sand irons), a reflection of Agatha's knowledge of, and familiarity with, the game.

The story *The Murder on the Links* has very little to do with golf and golf courses, apart from the fact that the body of the murdered Jack Renauld is found on the golf course, at a proposed site for what Poirot refers to as a 'bunkire', which he charmingly defines as, 'the irregular hole filled with sand and a bank at one side, is it not?'

Pets

Agatha was particularly attached to her dogs: the first being 'Toby', a Yorkshire terrier who was given as a present on her fifth birthday. Others included 'Joey', and a wire-haired terrier called 'Peter'. It is not surprising, therefore, that dogs found their way into her stories.

The appropriately named *Dumb Witness* for example, features a wire-haired terrier called 'Bob', which Agatha writes about in glowing terms. When Miss Emily Arundell has a fall, it is generally believed that this was caused by her tripping over a ball at the head of the stairs, placed there by Bob – it being his habit to bounce the ball down and catch it before it reached the bottom. However, Poirot discovers, that on the evening in question, Bob had taken himself out for the night, and that Miss Arundell had put his ball in a drawer. Therefore, the ball could not have been left at the top of the stairs. In fact, the would-be murderer had devised another method to cause Miss Arundell to trip and fall down them.

On the back cover of the book is displayed a picture of Bob with the humorous inscription: 'If it hadn't been for me, old Monsieur Poirot would never have solved this case. Bob – the *not* so dumb witness!'

15

Rosalind

Having been brought up by her mother Clara in an idiosyncratic, yet basically caring manner, Agatha now took her turn to rear a child, and she had certain definite and preconceived ideas as to how this should be done. One of her main concerns was for parents to realize that all children have their limitations, and they should therefore not be pressurized, in any way, to perform beyond their capabilities. For the child also, it was as well to realize, as early in life as possible, that there are certain things which cannot be achieved, and other things, which much as they want them, they could not have. Some parents were so desperately anxious for their offspring to do well, that they went so far as to tell them, openly, what enormous sacrifices they themselves had made in order for them to receive a good education. This is counter-productive, because on hearing these words, the child's reaction is to feel guilty if he or she fails to fulfil their expectations. Whereas, the general view was that if a child was to achieve, the key factor was opportunity. It was Agatha's view that he or she must also possess a natural aptitude for the job in hand. The parents of the late Victorian era were more sensible in their attitude, were more thoughtful for their children, and knew better what ingredients were necessary for them to enjoy life, and succeed in it. 'Keeping up with the Joneses' was a minor consideration. And finally, for the child who was not pressurized in this way, there was 'enormous relief' in not being asked to perform beyond their capabilities.[1]

On the other hand, as *The Case of the Missing Will* makes clear, Agatha was equally passionate that if children (in this case a daughter) do have potential, then they should be encouraged to fulfil it. The story involves

Miss Violet Marsh, an orphan, who is brought up by her uncle Andrew Marsh of Crabtree Manor, who has made a fortune in land speculation in Australia. Violet is Andrew's only blood relation. Although Andrew is a virtually uneducated person, he is strongly against women receiving an education. Matters come to a head when Violet wins a scholarship to Girton College, Cambridge. Whereupon, Andrew tells her that if she persists in these 'new-fangled notions' she can expect nothing from him in his will. When Andrew Marsh dies however, Crabtree Manor and its contents are placed at Violet's disposal for a period of one year, during the course of which, his 'clever niece may prove her wits'. If Violet fails so to do, then the entire estate and fortune will go to charity.

In fact, Violet does prove her wits, not by solving the puzzle of Andrew's will – which contains a conundrum that he has deliberately set for her – but by calling in Hercule Poirot to do it for her! In the words (albeit somewhat conceited ones) of the great man himself, to his colleague Captain Hastings, Miss Marsh had revealed the sharpness of her wits, and also the merits of higher education for women, by virtue of the fact that she had placed matters in *his* hands. The moral of the story, says Poirot, is 'Always employ the expert'.

When Rosalind's nanny Jessie Swannell fell out with Agatha's mother, she was replaced by an elderly, but incompetent nanny whom the family knew as 'Cuckoo'. She was a loving and kindly soul, said Agatha, but she mislaid everything, destroyed everything (presumably through carelessness and clumsiness), and made remarks that were so stupid as to be scarcely credible. She then goes on to give delightful descriptions of the interaction between Cuckoo and Rosalind, with Cuckoo continually fussing round the 'little dear', and Rosalind, in a role reversal, quietly taking charge by giving Cuckoo her instructions and finding items, such as a hair brush which Cuckoo had lost. It was somebody's duty, to maintain the nursery 'in a vague semblance of order', said Agatha, implying that that person was Rosalind, rather than Cuckoo![2]

However, behind the seemingly benign portrait of her relationship with Rosalind that Agatha paints in her autobiography, there is another story: one which is revealed in her semi-autobiographical novel *Unfinished Portrait*, where Rosalind is 'Judy'; Rosalind's mother is 'Celia'; and Rosalind's father is 'Dermot'. Just as Celia's mother Miriam, had seen her daughter as belonging particularly to her, so Celia saw her daughter

Judy, in the same light. To Celia, Judy was an adorable looking child, and yet she could see differences between herself and her daughter. For example, Celia had loved her mother to read stories to her, and as a result, she could remember, effortlessly, 'heaps' of such stories, and in particular, fairy stories, which she had particularly liked. Judy, on the other hand, had no interest in make-believe, and appeared to be lacking in imagination. As a girl, Celia could remember thinking of the lawn as an ocean, and her hoop a 'river horse'. But when she told Judy this, the latter simply saw the lawn as grass, and the hoop as something that one bowls, but does not ride. Not only that, but Judy gave her mother the impression that when she was a child, she must have been 'a rather silly little girl'. This was particularly deflating to Celia because she knew that Dermot felt the same way about her.

Judy was only 4 years old, and yet she had an immense amount of common sense, a fact that Celia often found depressing, because it had a bad effect on her. In her efforts to make Judy think she was sensible, Celia would often make a fool of herself. Judy was an enigma to her mother, and it disappointed Celia that all those pursuits in which she had loved to participate as a child, Judy found to be boring. Judy was unable to entertain herself in the garden, and was forever declaring how tedious life was. However, when she was inside the house, she enjoyed participating in the household chores, such as dusting, bed-making, and helping her father to clean his golf clubs.

It is abundantly clear that Celia was immensely fond of Judy. It is equally obvious that she found it difficult to accept that her daughter was different in character from herself. Whereas Celia was sensitive, imaginative, and creative, Judy was down to earth, realistic, 'sensible'. It was, therefore, not surprising that Judy failed to appreciate the same things that Agatha had so enjoyed as a child. As for the family home (an allusion, of course, to Ashfield), Celia doubted whether Judy cherished it as she had done - but, on the other hand, why should she? Judy, to Celia's way of thinking, was 'aloof' and 'unattached', just like her father Dermot. People like them inhabited dwellings simply as a convenience.

Judy's relationship with Dermot was again, something which Celia was puzzled by, if not jealous of. The two of them had become friends, and a 'satisfying communion' existed between them. Dermot, even though he was somewhat critical of Judy's tendency to chubbiness, was charmed by her company, just as she relished his. The two of them were able to converse easily, and hold serious conversations, just like adults. When it came to Judy cleaning his golf clubs, Dermot was a hard taskmaster, and insisted on her making a thorough job of it. When she, in turn, asked him to admire something that she had made, he gave her a frank opinion and was not slow to point out her faults. Celia feared that Judy would become discouraged by Dermot's critical attitude, but this proved not to be the case, and she sustained no hurt to her feelings. It was *because* she found her father harder to please that she liked him more than her mother. She was a child who *preferred* to accept challenges that were difficult, rather than taking the easy way out.

Celia noticed that whenever the two of them played together, Judy nearly always ended up with some sort of injury, on account of Dermot's roughness. Judy seemed unaffected by this; neither was she deterred from preferring robust games to tame ones. Only in times of illness did Judy appear to favour her mother, rather than her father. Then she would beg her mother not to go away. This state of affairs suited Dermot perfectly well. He would have preferred it if people had not been ill. Such things as illness and unhappiness were merely an embarrassment to him.

Something else that Judy and Dermot had in common was that neither of them liked being touched. Judy could tolerate a single good-night kiss from her mother at bedtime, but nothing more. As for Dermot, he never kissed Judy, and at night-time, the two of them simply grinned at one another. Sometimes, Celia was surprised by what Judy said. For example, during a conversation about kindness, in relation to the beloved family dog Aubrey, she suddenly said to her mother, 'You're kind – you're very kind. Daddy's not kind, but he's very, very jolly…'. On another occasion, she informed Celia smugly, that Dermot did not like her much, but in contrast, he did like *her*.

Agatha's bewilderment – revealed by her through the character 'Celia' – is obvious. Here was the child Judy (Rosalind) she had always longed for, but she was poised, self-confidant, perhaps a little conceited, manipulative even. The word 'insecurity' did not enter into her vocabulary. For Judy (and for her own daughter Rosalind), there was no nightmarish 'Gunman', waiting in the wings, threatening to shatter her childhood dreams, as there had been for Agatha.

Judy was not interested in listening to stories (even though Agatha mentions that Rosalind, as a very young child, *did* enjoy them). She disdained the cuddles which Celia (Agatha) would have liked to give her, behaved maturely, like an adult, and made Celia, who wished to share her childhood pastimes with her, feel 'silly'. Judy was, like children often are, disarmingly honest. She said what she felt, and took from each parent what suited her best. But for Celia, most hurtful of all was the fact that she seemed to identify much more with her father Dermot (Archie): enjoying his company, doing things with him, rather than with her mother, and finally telling Celia what she most dreaded to hear – that her father Dermot did not like her.

16

Literary Success but Problems Loom

A friend of Archie's, Major E.A. Belcher, invited him to be his financial adviser on a 9 month journey round the world, designed to enlist
support for the forthcoming British Empire Mission to be held in 1924
at Wembley, London. Agatha could accompany them, and perhaps this
would help to cement the couple's relationship. In the meantime, daughter Rosalind would be looked after by Agatha's mother Clara, and by her
sister Madge – who now had a second nickname – 'Auntie Punkie'.

The party set off on 20 January 1922 for Cape Town, aboard the Union
Castle Line vessel RMS *Kildonan Castle*, whereupon Agatha was terribly
seasick. Among the places they would visit would be the diamond mines
at Kimberley, Southern Rhodesia's Matopos Hills, the Victoria Falls, and
Johannesburg and Durban. Another sea voyage took them to Australia
and Tasmania. But it was New Zealand that Agatha, not one to shrink
from the use of the superlative, described as 'the most beautiful country'
that she had ever seen.[1]

In Honolulu, Agatha learnt to surf, and described a 'moment of complete triumph', when she managed to keep her balance and sail her surf
board right up onto the beach without falling off it. Then it was on to
New York and Canada, where she said Lake Louise was 'the most beautiful place' that she had ever seen.[2] Major Belcher would subsequently
feature in *The Mystery of the Mill House* (later renamed *The Man in the
Brown Suit*) which was set partly in South Africa, with Belcher appearing
in the guise of the fictitious 'Sir Eustace Pedler'. This, she believed, was
the one and only time that she had attempted to transform a real-life
character, whom she knew, into a character in a book, and she regretted
to say that she did not think the experiment had been a success.[3]

When the couple arrived home from their world tour they found themselves in dire financial straits. Agatha wanted herself and Archie to share the hardship together. Archie however, suggested that she went home to her mother, which she refused to do. Finally, with the idea of bringing in some money, Agatha decided to resume her writing, although even then she said she still had no thoughts of becoming a writer.[4]

When Rosalind's nanny 'Cuckoo', developed breast cancer and was forced to leave the household, she was replaced by a Miss White – which Rosalind pronounced 'Swite'. In these times of austerity it appears that Agatha and Swite shared responsibility for the cooking. Unfortunately, said Agatha, neither had any notion of how to produce what is normally called 'a balanced meal'. In preparing a joint and the various vegetables which went with it, together with a dessert to follow, they were handicapped in that they did not know how much time these various items took to cook.[5]

When *Murder on the Links* was accepted by the Bodley Head, they offered Agatha a contract for a total of five books. She declined their offer, and at the suggestion of Edmund Cork, who had succeeded Hughes Massie as her literary agent, placed herself in the hands of publishers William Collins Sons & Co. Ltd. Meanwhile, *The Evening News* offered to serialize *The Mystery of the Mill House*.

Archie, for his part, joined the firm of an Australian friend Clive Baillieu, where, in Agatha's words, 'he was immediately, wonderfully, completely happy'. The family, including Swite, now moved to a flat in Sunningdale, Berkshire (part of a large house called 'Scotswood'), Archie having been elected to the golf club there. Agatha was now dismayed on two counts: firstly, she had hoped to move further into the country but this had not happened, and secondly, she was unable to share in Archie's love of golf. He could derive no enjoyment from playing with a novice such as she was, she said, and soon found that she had become, 'that well-known figure, a golf widow'.[6]

With her increasing success on the literary front, which included the serialization of *Anna the Adventuress* in *The Evening News*, Agatha was able, at Archie's suggestion, to purchase a Morris Cowley motor car. (Not only did the vehicle give her enormous pleasure, it also proved useful for transporting Archie to Hounslow Station, for him to catch the train to London during the General Strike of 1926).

By now, the realization was beginning to come to Agatha that perhaps one day, she *might* become a writer by profession. However, she bewailed the fact that she received but little encouragement from Archie when it came to constructing plots for her new books. She also composed songs, and set some of her poems, and also some verses from Pierrot and Harlequin (traditional figures from Italian Comedy) to music.[7]

On this rollercoaster of 'ups' and 'downs', there now came another series of 'downs' for Agatha, who described her weekends as her 'dullest time'. She would have liked to entertain guests, but Archie said that this would spoil his weekends. The presence of people in the house would require him to spend more time at home, and he would, therefore, miss his second round of golf of the day, said Agatha. The problem was, to some extent, solved however, when her sister-in-law Nan Kon (*née* Watts) and Nan's second husband George came to stay: the two men played golf together, while she and Nan talked, and indulged in, 'some desultory golf on the ladies' links'.[8]

When Swite left, she was replaced by a Swiss governess Marcelle Vignou. For Rosalind this was not a success and she began to misbehave. Agatha now decided to employ a combined secretary-cum-governess. When Rosalind reached the age of five she would attend school each morning, during which time Agatha's secretary, who would be skilled at shorthand-typing, would be at her service. It might even be that she could dictate her literary creations, rather than write the manuscripts out in longhand. When the post was duly filled by Miss Charlotte Fisher, nicknamed 'Carlo', Rosalind's behaviour improved, and she rapidly reverted to her former self.[9] Meanwhile, *The Murder of Roger Ackroyd*, featuring, for the first time, the female sleuth Miss Jane Marple, was published by William Collins.

The family dog Joey, had died while Agatha and Archie had been abroad with Major Belcher. Now, Rosalind was given the present of a wire-haired terrier puppy who was given the name Peter.[10] He would sleep on Carlo's bed, having eaten his way through several pairs of slippers, and destroyed special balls which were supposed to be indestructible as far as terriers were concerned.[11] Troubled times were fast approaching, when even though Peter was technically Rosalind's dog, Agatha would greatly appreciate having him as a companion.

When Agatha suggested to Archie that they might have another baby, Archie dismissed the idea at once. He wanted no one but Rosalind. Rosalind was 'absolutely satisfactory', and quite sufficient for him. Archie, now the proud owner of a second-hand Delage motor car, was convinced that their present location, Sunningdale, was the ideal place in which to reside, especially because of its proximity to the newly opened Wentworth Golf Course. The couple, therefore, proceeded to purchase the first house of their own which they called 'Styles', since in Agatha's words, the first of her books which had brought her 'a stake in life', had been *The Mysterious Affair at Styles*.[12]

On 5 April 1926, Agatha's mother Clara died at the age of seventy-two. Although Agatha would clearly have liked Archie to be there, her husband was unable to attend the funeral as he was in Spain at the time. In any case, said Agatha, he had a violent antipathy towards illness, death, and 'trouble of any kind'.[13] When Archie returned to England, he remained at his club in London, whilst Agatha returned to Torquay, to her family home Ashfield. Agatha could not bear to part with the house, and decided that when she had sorted out her late mother's belongings, it would be let.

Archie's failure to give moral support in Agatha's time of sorrow is made clear in her novel *Unfinished Portrait*, in which Celia (Agatha's counterpart) describes her husband Dermot (i.e. Archie) as inadequate, someone who was persistently unable to empathize with the 'emotional stress' of others; someone who 'shied away from it like a frightened horse'. And yet Celia (Agatha) wrestles with her emotions, saying that in theory, Dermot meant to be kind, and even wanted to be kind, but that in practice, he was unkind. She now felt afraid. How sterile the world seemed to be in the absence of her mother.

Meanwhile, Dermot wrote her only infrequently, and when he did, his letters were short and their content referred, mainly, to his most recent game of golf: where he had played; how many strokes he had taken for his round; whom he had played with; how he had got Marjorie Connell to make up a fourth – despite the fact that he had always declared women to be a nuisance on the golf course. (In *Unfinished Portrait*, 'Marjorie Connell' becomes Dermot's mistress, just as in real life Nancy Neele became Archie's mistress).

Now came another blow: Carlo left the household to attend to her father who had become very ill with cancer. Agatha bade her a tearful farewell. She was now afflicted by a sense of utter loneliness, exacerbated by Archie's rejection of her suggestion that he should come to visit her for the occasional weekend.[14] When Archie did, finally, come down to Ashfield, all it did was to make her remember the 'old nightmare' which she had suffered as a child: the horrifying feeling of sitting up at the tea table, looking across at my dearest friend – perhaps her mother – with the sudden realization that it was not the person whom she believed it to be, but *'a stranger'*.[15] (In other words, Agatha's husband had seemingly been replaced by a stranger, just as in her childhood nightmares the 'Gunman' had threatened to replace her mother). The truth was that Archie had fallen in love with Miss Nancy Neele, a fellow golfer (who, incidentally, had formerly been secretary to Major E.A. Belcher, whom Agatha and Archie had accompanied on the world tour.)

And what of Rosalind ('Judy' in *Unfinished Portrait*)? Whereas Dermot confessed, that as far as his daughter was concerned, he did have regrets about the break-up of the marriage, nevertheless, it was his understanding that he and Celia had each agreed that 'the other should be perfectly free…'. Celia had no recollection of this, but Dermot persisted, saying that to his way of thinking, this was the only 'decent' way to view a marriage. Celia now remonstrates with him, saying that when a couple have conceived a child, the decent thing would be to remain with it. Dermot, however, was not to be moved.

Into her writing-case, Agatha, in a symbolic gesture of separation – albeit an unwilling one on her part – placed the wedding ring Archie had given her, together with some letters from him, various momentos, and a copy of Psalm 55, verses 12, 13 and 14, which, with its poignant words, summed up precisely her feelings of deep hurt:

> For it is not an open enemy, that hath done me
> this dishonour: for then I could have borne it.
> Neither was it mine adversary, that did magnify
> himself against me: for then peradventure I
> would have hid myself from him.
> But it was even thou, my companion: my guide, and
> mine own familiar friend.[16]

It was extraordinary, how, in the midst of all this mental trauma, Agatha's creative instincts for writing could have survived; but remain intact they did, and with financial problems looming once more, she decided to write another book. It would be entitled *The Mystery of the Blue Train*. Agatha described this as the moment when she metamorphosed from being an amateur to being a professional, which she defined as feeling obliged to write, even in moments when one does not wish to.

Agatha now derived some small comfort from the providential return of Carlo; the doctors having declared that her father was not suffering from cancer after all…[17] As secretary-cum-shorthand-typist, Carlo could now resume her duties and assist Agatha in her next project.

17

Unfinished Portrait: Agatha in Depth

As previously mentioned, Agatha's novel *Unfinished Portrait*, published in the year 1934 under the pseudonym 'Mary Westmacott', is in fact semi-autobiographical. Ostensibly, it is the story of Celia, as recounted by Larraby, a portrait painter.

The two of them had met overseas on an island, at a time when Celia was contemplating suicide, having lost the three people who were most dear to her: her mother, her husband, and her daughter. Now, despite the fact that the chance of happiness beckons for her once more, she finds herself facing a dilemma. She lacks the courage to face life on her own, and yet she dreads the thought of committing herself to any possible future partner.

The sentiments expressed above by Celia are, in reality, an in-depth description by Agatha of this unhappy period, and a far more candid one than is provided by her autobiography.

When, in *Unfinished Portrait*, Celia's father dies, she is reminded of the night terrors from which she suffered as a child. Everything was satisfactory until The Gun Man made his presence felt, and when he did appear on the scene, unexpected and untoward things could happen. Tears came into her eyes.

This is Agatha, who at the same period of her life as Celia, was terrified of change; reliving her feelings on the death of her own father Frederick. (Incidentally, whereas in Agatha's autobiography she speaks of 'The Gunman', in *Unfinished Portrait* it is 'The Gun Man'.)

Agatha's mother Clara's ('Miriam' in the novel) reservations about Archie Christie are also mirrored in the novel. Yes, she did like him, she even considered him to be 'very attractive indeed', but what worried her was that he was inconsiderate...

However, despite her mother's warning, Celia marries Dermot (who, like Archie, served on the Western Front in the First World War), and inevitably, cracks soon begin to appear. In her married life, Celia suffered above all from a feeling of loneliness. (By which she meant both physical and emotional). Now Agatha bares her soul, and in what must have been a catharsis for her, she describes (reliving her experiences vicariously through her character 'Celia') in detail the preamble to what was to be the most traumatic period of her life.

Celia knew full well that there were many aspects to her character that Dermot disliked: her 'helplessness' being one of them. Why did Celia want him to do things for her, when she was perfectly capable of doing them for herself? When Celia declares that it would be nice if Dermot offered her the occasional helping hand, he tells her that as a person who was 'perfectly sensible', 'intelligent', and 'capable', she ought to be able to manage on her own. When Celia confesses that she feels an automatic need to cling to him 'like ivy', Dermot puts his foot down. She would not cling to him. He would not allow it.

Celia was a person who loved to share, and when the almond tree came into flower, she would have loved to have taken Dermot's hand, shown it to him, and enjoyed the experience with him. Dermot, however, disliked not only holding hands, but being touched in any way at all, except for the occasions when he made it clear that he was in the mood for romance. When Celia singed her hand on the kitchen stove, and pinched her finger whilst closing a window, she would have loved to have nestled her head on Dermot's shoulder and sought comfort there. She refrained, however, knowing that this would annoy him as he simply could not 'enter into other peoples' emotions'. The result is, that she has to fight a constant battle with herself, by not revealing her desire to share, to be caressed, and to be reassured; telling herself, that in so doing she is being 'babyish and foolish'.

When Celia tells Dermot that she believes she is pregnant, his reply is that he does not want a baby. And why? Because it would take up all of Celia's time, and he would be left out. This was invariably the case with women. When they were being 'domestic', and 'messing about with a baby', it was their habit to forget about their husbands completely.

This, surely, is a reflection of Archie's jealous feelings, as he anticipates how a future offspring might become a rival to himself for his wife Agatha's attentions.

When (like Archie), Dermot makes it clear that he wishes to play golf every weekend, Celia complains bitterly. She looked forward with great anticipation to their weekends together. She loved his company. And now she feared that they would not share in doing anything together ever again. Here again, Dermot is mirroring Archie's obsession with the game of golf.

In Chapter 17 of *Unfinished Portrait*, entitled *Disaster*, Celia asks Dermot whether there is anything the matter. She felt frightened, sick with terror, and yet she could not account for it. Was it really his intention to leave them, and not see either her his wife, or Judy their daughter, any more? But Dermot was Judy's father, she told him reproachfully, and Judy loved him.

In Chapter 18, entitled *Fear*, Celia reveals in harrowing detail her reaction when Dermot (Archie) demands a divorce. At night, she would wake up feeling utterly terrified; convinced that Dermot was trying to poison her in order to remove her from the scene. She would often wander about during the night time, looking for something, but not knowing what it was. Then one day, she realized that she was looking for her mother. She, therefore, put on her clothes, and taking a photograph of her mother with her, went to the police station to see if they could trace Miriam. Celia was sure that the police would eventually find her, and once her mother had been found 'everything would be alright...'. Finally, Celia recovers her senses. How foolish she had been. How *could* she have found her mother, when her mother was *dead*? Again, this is really Agatha's voice, revealing how, in this supreme moment of crisis, she longs for the love, comfort, and stability which her mother could have provided, had she still been alive.

During her marital difficulties, Celia describes how Dermot's face had reminded her of something – not something, but someone – The Gun Man, who gave her a feeling of horror. She now realized that during all the time of her marital difficulties, Dermot had 'really' been The Gun Man. This made her feel sick with fear. She must go home, hide away. The Gun Man was seeking her out. Dermot was 'stalking her down...'.

(It should be remembered, however, that Agatha, at the time of her own divorce from Archie, had long since grown out of her childhood night terrors, even though the memory of them remained etched on her mind.)

When Miss Hood (Carlo in real life) called in the doctor to attend to Celia, the advice given by him, in a firm but kindly way, was for her to place herself in Miss Hood's capable hands, which she did. As for Miss

Hood, she willingly donned the mantle of responsibility, being careful, wherever possible, never to leave Celia and Dermot alone together. Now Celia could cling to the kindly Miss Hood with whom she felt safe.

So Agatha, who is still mourning the death of her beloved mother, is now obliged to contemplate a further blow: the loss of husband and home. The strain is too great. Something surely has to give – and very soon it does. Only in her novel *Unfinished Portrait*, is the true extent of Agatha's grief revealed.

Celia now realized that she was alone, and that her husband Dermot, and her daughter Judy were strangers to her. She also bewailed the fact that there was no one to whom she could go to seek comfort any more, which presumably was a reference to her late mother Miriam. First, she felt a sense of panic, which was followed by remorse: this, because she had been so preoccupied with Dermot and Judy over the last few years, that she had given her mother little thought, even though the latter had always been there for her, in the background. The two of them knew each other, intimately. 'Wonderful' and 'satisfying', was how Celia described her relationship with her mother when she had been a small child. Now that her mother was gone, her world had collapsed. She felt herself shivering. How she longed to be free, with no encumbrances such as belongings, properties, a husband, or children to hold her back, to tie her down, to pull at her heart strings. How she desired to run away!

Agatha Disappears

On 3 December 1926, Agatha disappeared for 11 days, her whereabouts remaining unknown, despite a nationwide police search. She was now aged thirty-six. The event caused considerable interest and gave rise to much speculation. The world's most famous mystery writer had herself become the subject of mystery!

On the morning of Saturday, 4 December 1926, the day after Agatha's disappearance, her motor car was discovered in a remote lane in Surrey, 2 miles east of the city of Guildford, and 12 miles south-east of her home Styles, at Sunningdale, Berkshire. What could have possessed her to abandon her precious Morris Cowley, her pride and joy; the acquisition of which she would one day describe as being a highlight in her life? Or on the other hand, could she have been abducted? *The Times* newspaper, along with many others, was swiftly on to the case, and carried the following report:

Frederick Dore, of Alexander Road, Thames Ditton, who found the car abandoned near Newlands Corner on Saturday morning, said yesterday that he found in it a fur coat, a case, and some other things… When he found the car the brakes were off, and it was in neutral [gear]. The running board and the under part of the carriage were resting on the bushes. The position of the car suggested to him that it must have been given a push at the top of the hill and sent down deliberately. The lights were off and had evidently been left on until the current became exhausted. If anyone had accidentally run off the road the car would have been pulled up earlier. There was no sign that the brakes had been applied.[1]

A description given by the *Harrogate Advertiser* provided even more graphic details. The motor car, it said, was found:

near a chalk pit a few hundred yards below Newlands Corner. [In contrast, Superintendent William Kenward, Deputy Chief Constable of the Surrey Constabulary, describes 'the numerous gravel pits that abound there,' rather than chalk pits].[2] The car appeared as though it had run down from the corner with the brakes off, and gathering speed, had swerved off into a thick hedge and become lodged there, the front wheels overhanging the edge of the chalk pit.[3]

In his report to the Home Office, Superintendent Kenward also stated that the vehicle:

was found in such a position as to indicate that some unusual proceeding had taken place, the Car being found half-way down a grassy slope well off the road with its bonnet buried in some bushes, as if it had got out of control.[4]

On 7 December 1926, *The Times* newspaper reported that the previous evening, a man (Edward McAlister) had:

come forward who says that about an hour before dawn on Saturday morning [4 December] he was approached by a woman at Newlands Corner, who asked him to start her car. The car had evidently been out in the frost all night, and the woman's hair – she was hatless – was covered with hoarfrost. She appeared to be strange in her manner. With considerable difficulty the man started the engine of the car, and the woman drove off in the direction of Clandon. It was about two hours later that the car was discovered abandoned near the spot from which she was seen to drive away.

On the afternoon of 7 December 1926, two aeroplanes joined in the search. That day, the newspapers carried a police description of Agatha, describing her as being of:

Height 5ft. 7in., hair reddish and shingled [a type of hair cut], eyes grey, complexion fair, well built, dressed in grey stockinet skirt, green jumper, grey and dark-grey cardigan, small green velour hat, wearing a platinum ring with one pearl. No wedding ring [which of course is highly significant, given the circumstances]. Had black handbag with her, containing probably £5 to £10.

On 8 December, *The Times* elaborated on the story which it had carried the previous day:

Edward McAlister of Merrow, who told the police on Monday night that he helped a lady motorist to start her car near Newlands Corner on Saturday morning [4 December – see above], made a statement on the subject yesterday. He said that about 400 yards from the top of Newlands Corner, on the road leading over Merrow Downs, he saw a grey car. A lady came out from behind the car and asked if he would start it. The radiator was quite cold. The woman had no coat or hat on, and was wearing a grey jumper. After some time he got the car started, and the woman drove the car very slowly away down hill towards Merrow and away from Newlands Corner. If that was the car that was abandoned, the woman must have turned round and driven up the hill behind him. He could see nobody else about.

When interviewed by Superintendent Kenward, McAlister gave the time when he helped Agatha to start the car as 6.20a.m. 'McAlister stated also that this lady was very sparsely dressed for such an inclement morning, and that she appeared strange in her manner.'[5] (There were many other reported sightings of Agatha, which have been ignored in this text as they do not appear to fit with the proven facts).

Superintendent Kenward gave his reasons for concentrating the search in the vicinity of the downs around Newlands Corner. This was because of 'the disquieting nature of certain information that had come to my knowledge…'.[6] What could this information have been, and what was its source?

On 10 December 1926, the *Daily Mail* newspaper gave an update on the events of the previous day:

Organised in two main [search] parties and under the direction of Supt. Kenward…, Supt. Bosher of Woking, and Supt. Port of Godalming, one [search party] worked from the direction of Dorking towards Newlands Corner, near where Mrs Christie's abandoned motor-car was found, and the other from Guildford.

They met at Newlands Corner at dusk to-night, a weary body of men, after searching the Downs and woods and gorseland for seven hours. Meanwhile a small party searched in and around Newlands Corner. The whole search has proved fruitless. Not the slightest clue has been found.

Husband Archie had also participated in the search:

For three hours this afternoon [7 December], Col. Christie with his wife's favourite wire-haired terrier Peter, and accompanied by Supt. Kenward, searched every bush near the spot where the abandoned car was found. But the whimpering dog could find no trace of its mistress.

An aeroplane again took part in the search and a caterpillar tractor from Ewhurst tore up bushes and thick hedges, while scores of dogs ran into swamps, all with negative results.

'I have handled many important cases during my career,' Superintendent Kenward told me [i.e. told the *Daily Mail's* special correspondent] when the search was over, 'but this is the most baffling mystery ever [to be] set me for solution.'

The newspaper then intimated that the superintendent would travel to London the following day with the intention of consulting Scotland Yard. This statement, however, was refuted by Superintendent Kenward, who declared that, 'The police engaged in the search were not drawn from other Counties, as was suggested, neither were the Metropolitan Police called in.'[7] Said the *Daily Mail*:

Despite the fruitless character of the day's work, Superintendent Kenward still believes that the solution of the mystery lies near Newlands Corner and not far from where the car was found.[8]

The newspaper headlines of the time reveal the enormous public interest in the case, and the strenuous efforts that were devoted to the solving of it: '500 POLICE SEARCH FOR MRS CHRISTIE' (*Daily Mail*); 'THE MISSING WOMAN NOVELIST: POLICE WORKING ON NEW INFORMATION: AEROPLANES USED FOR THE FIRST TIME' (*The Times*). (There is no doubt that aeroplanes were seen overhead during the search, but as Superintendent Kenward states, these were, 'nothing to do with the police.'[9])

The involvement of the public was huge, with 2,000 civilian volunteers, local huntsmen and hounds, and individual owners of bloodhounds being enlisted to search for Agatha, the area around her home at Sunningdale in Berkshire also receiving attention:

> The Downs in the vicinity of her [Agatha's] home have been searched repeatedly and on Sunday [December 12], it was said that 1,000 people were engaged in the task, including police, special constables and civilians. The woods were searched, and a mill pond at Albury was dragged, but without result. [10]

Former Chief Inspector Gough, late of Scotland Yard, summed up the situation thus:

> Mrs Christie has, wittingly or unwittingly, in real life been the central figure in a mystery that surpasses anything in her clever novels. [11]

The Mystery Deepens

In a statement to the *Daily Mail* newspaper, Archie, referring to 3 December 1926, the day of his wife Agatha's disappearance, had this to say:

> I left home at 9.15a.m. in the ordinary way and that was the last time I saw my wife. I knew that she had arranged to go to Yorkshire for the week-end. I understand that in the morning she went motoring and then lunched alone. In the afternoon she went [with Rosalind] to see my mother [Rosamund Hemsley – who had remarried after the death of her husband Archibald Christie senior] at Dorking.

What was the purpose of Agatha's visit to her mother-in-law's house Middle Lodge, Deepdene, Dorking, Surrey? Was it simply a social call, or was there a more serious motive on Agatha's part? Did she, in fact, intend to make a last ditch appeal to Mrs Hemsley to intercede in her marital problems, by persuading her son Archie to give up Nancy Neele and return to her? And did she take Rosalind with her as a kind of bargaining counter, there to reinforce the fact that Archie, by his actions, was turning his back not just on Agatha, but on his daughter also? Archie continued:

> She [Agatha] returned here [to Sunningdale] in time for dinner, which she took alone. I do not know what happened after that…

That evening, when Archie failed to return home, Agatha put her daughter Rosalind to bed, before driving off into the night. Only the parlour-maid and the cook remained in the house, Carlo (Charlotte Fisher), her secretary, being absent on a day trip to London. However, according to Archie, Agatha:

left a note addressed to Miss Fisher [who returned home to Styles at 11p. m.], in which she asked for the arrangements for the Yorkshire visit that weekend [which she and Archie had apparently intended to make] to be cancelled, adding that she was going for a run round [in the car] and would let her know on the morrow where she was.[1]

According to the *Daily Mail*, the contents of this letter:

were revealed to the police, who kept them a close secret. The letter was placed under seal... Whatever its contents were, they apparently convinced Superintendent Kenward... that she [Agatha] would be found, probably dead from exposure or otherwise, somewhere in the wild country in that neighbourhood.[2]

This letter then, was apparently the source of the 'disquieting information' to which Superintendent Kenward referred in his statement to the Home Office.[3] The implication is clear. The letter left by Agatha for Carlo led the police to believe that on that December night, Agatha set out from home in her car with the deliberate intention of committing suicide. Could this be true? It would be over a year before the answer to this question was forthcoming, and it was supplied by Agatha herself. (Agatha also left a letter for Archie, which he destroyed without revealing its contents).

On 8 December 1926, the following article appeared in *The Times* newspaper:

It was learnt, late last night, that a brother of Colonel Christie, living in London, had received a letter written by the missing woman [i.e. Agatha] since her disappearance, and that in it she stated that she was in ill-health and was going to a Yorkshire spa. The Surrey police, however, had communicated with certain centres in Yorkshire, and as a result are satisfied, it is understood, that Mrs Christie is not in that county.

On 9 December 1926, *The Times* reported:

Every effort is being made to throw light upon the letter from Mrs Christie, which her brother-in-law received after her disappearance [see above]. The postmark on the envelope was well defined, and enquiries were made in the 'SW1' postal district in the hope of discovering the sender of the letter.

On Friday 10 December 1926 (it now being a week since Agatha's disappearance) the *Daily Mail*'s Special Correspondent reported that:

> Friends of Mrs Christie have told me today [9 December] that recently she has been particularly depressed, and that on one occasion she said, 'If I do not leave Sunningdale, Sunningdale will be the end of me.'

The same day, the *Daily Mail* also published a statement, given to them by Archie, of his views on the fate which may have befallen his wife:

> It is quite true that my wife had discussed the possibility of disappearing at will. Some time ago she told her sister, 'I could disappear if I wished [to] and set about it carefully.'[4]
>
> Personally I feel that is what happened. At any rate, I am buoying myself up with that belief. You see, there are three possible explanations of her disappearance: Voluntary, Loss of memory, and Suicide. I am inclined to the first, although, of course, it may be loss of memory as a result of her highly nervous state.
>
> I do not believe this is a case of suicide. She never threatened suicide, but if she did contemplate that, I am sure her mind would turn to poison. I do not mean that she has ever discussed the question of taking poison, but that she used poison very largely in her stories.
>
> I have remonstrated with her in regard to this form of death [presumably a reference to Agatha's use of this device in her stories, which Archie evidently did not approve of], but her mind always turned to it. If she wanted to get poison, I am sure she could have done so. She was very clever at getting anything she wanted.
>
> But against the theory of suicide you have to remember this: if a person intends to end his life [or in this case her life] he does not take the trouble to go miles away and then remove a heavy coat and then walk off into the blue before doing it. [This was a reference to the fact that Agatha had left her fur coat behind in the car, when she abandoned it at Newlands Corner.]

From this, it appears that Archie had nothing to offer which would shed light on the subject, except to assert that he believed Agatha still to be alive.

Agatha is Found

It was not until Tuesday, 14 December 1926 that Agatha's whereabouts finally became known, and when it did, this was not as a result of the police investigation, but rather because of the observant eyes of two musicians who worked at the Hydropathic Hotel, situated in the spa town of Harrogate in Yorkshire – or as it was commonly known, 'The Hydro'. Under the heading 'THE MEN WHO RECOGNISED MRS CHRISTIE', the local newspaper, the *Harrogate Advertiser*, gave the following intriguing and astonishing account of events leading up to Agatha's discovery:

Mr Robert H. Tappin and Mr Robert W. Leeming, two members of the dance orchestra [of The Hydro], gave the information to the police which led to Mrs Christie's identification. They were both attracted to her by her awkward manner, even on the day of her arrival, but did not become suspicious until a week later.

In an interview, Mr Tappin, who plays the banjo in the band, and also sings in the Sunday concerts, said that on the night of Saturday December 4th, he noticed Mrs Christie in the ballroom. 'There was something about her which made her stand out apart from the other guests. Her dress and her demeanour were different, and she seemed rather awkward. I was particularly interested in the case, because I come from the neighbourhood of Newlands Corner. On Sunday, at the social function in the lounge, she sang something from *Samson and Delilah* [opera by Saint-Saëns], and I noticed a strong resemblance to Mrs Christie. Again, on the following Saturday, when we were playing, I saw her, and was more impressed because I had in the meantime studied all the photographs I could get. I was singing at the concert and she was also singing. I sat next to her and studied her as much as I could. One of the songs she sang was *Softly Awakes my Heart* in French. She also sang a song to her own accompaniment, which greatly impressed me, because she appeared to know it thoroughly. The song was *I once loved a Boy, a Bonny, Bonny Boy*, and I thought it would be a good clue if her husband knew it was one of her favourite songs. She also asked for *Up from Somerset*. I gave this, and also *Drake goes West*, and she seemed thoroughly to enjoy them. Mrs Christie, who sang most of the songs to her own accompaniment, tried another song, lent by Miss Corbett, the lady entertainer, but she broke down and laughingly said she did not know it.

When I went home, I said to Bob Leeming, who is with me in the band, that the likeness to Mrs Christie was very marked. He also noted it, and we got out all the [news] papers and studied the photographs. We were then so sure of the fact that we decided to inform the police of our suspicions...'

It was also reported that 'Mr R.W. Leeming [Bob], who plays the saxophone in the band, said that he thought Mrs Christie seemed a bit eccentric'.

The story was covered both by the *Harrogate Advertiser*, and by another local newspaper, the *Harrogate Herald*:

Discreet enquiries were made, so as not to make the lady suspicious, and the result of this was that Supt. G.A. McDowall communicated with the Surrey police on Tuesday morning [14 December]. Col. Christie was informed of the clue, and he immediately left for Harrogate, arriving there at about half past six [p.m.][1]

Having met with Superintendent McDowall at Harrogate police station, Archie and he:

proceeded by car to The Hydro. They took up a position in the lounge, and Col. Christie was obviously labouring under great strain. Mrs Christie was dressing for dinner, and they had over half an hour to wait before she put in an appearance. She walked down the stairs instead of [taking] the lift...[2]

When Col. Christie arrived it was arranged he should sit in the lounge and await Mrs Christie as she came down to dinner. He took up a newspaper, behind which he hid, and when his wife appeared he immediately recognised her.[3]

At this juncture, it is pertinent to enquire as to what specifically triggered Agatha's flight? Could it have been some event which occurred immediately beforehand, perhaps on the morning of Friday, 3 December 1926? This possibility was refuted by Archie, who on 9 December 1926 told the *Daily Mail's* Special Correspondent:

> It is absolutely untrue to suggest that there was anything in the nature of a row or tiff between my wife and myself on Friday morning [3 December]. She was perfectly well – that is to say, as well as she had been for months past. She knew I was going away for the week-end: she knew who were going to be the members of the little party at the house of [in] which I was going to stay, and neither then nor at any time did she raise the slightest objection.[3]

This account of Archie's is at variance with the impression given by Agatha in her novel *Unfinished Portrait*, which strongly implies that there was, in fact, a forthright exchange of views between herself and Archie on that morning, on the subject of Archie ('Dermot' in the novel) continuing to see his mistress Nancy Neele ('Marjorie Connell'), even though he had promised not to.

What Archie also omitted to say in his statement to the *Daily Mail* was that he intended to spend the weekend of Agatha's disappearance at Hurstmore Cottage, Godalming (4 miles south of Guildford). This was the home of Sam James (a colleague of Archie's in the City) and his wife Madge, who had also invited Archie's mistress Nancy Neele (whose family home was at Croxley Green, near Watford in Hertfordshire).[4] When challenged, Archie did not deny it, or that he had previously spent many previous weekends away from home, presumably in the company of Nancy Neele; a fact about which Agatha was almost certainly painfully aware.

With regard to potentially stressful lifetime events, bereavement, especially one which involves a close relation, and marital break-up rate particularly highly. Agatha was obliged to endure both in the space of a few short months: first, when her beloved mother Clara died, which took a heavy toll, as her secretary Carlo indicated; secondly, as her own marital problems rose inexorably to their climax. The argument with Archie on the morning of Friday, 3 December, appears to have been the final straw which left Agatha, in her own mind, no choice but to pursue a course of self-destruction.

On Wednesday 15 December, the *Daily Mail*'s Special Correspondent reported that he himself:

> was the first person to convey the definite news of Mrs Christie's discovery to Styles, her home… Miss Fisher [Carlo], her secretary… was delighted. 'Thank God for that!' was her first remark. 'It is splendid.' [She then added] Mrs Christie has been in ill-health for a very considerable time. She felt very keenly the loss of her mother. It preyed upon her so because they had never been separated until Mrs Miller died.

Another *Daily Mail* reporter was the first to inform Mrs Hemsley, Agatha's mother-in-law at Dorking. Her response was:

> Oh, how poor Agatha must have suffered! Her mind must have been a complete blank. Even now I cannot really think that she can be alive. I know her so well that I refuse to believe that she did not lose her memory. She would not live in an hotel on her own, fully alive to all this fuss and anxiety she was causing, not sending a word even to her own relatives.[5]

So how had Agatha occupied herself during her time at The Hydro? In fact, when this period of her life is examined and evaluated, it becomes evident that even more questions are raised than are answered.

Agatha's Own Story

Just over a year later, on 16 February 1928, Agatha gave a full and frank account to the *Daily Mail* of the events leading up to and including her famous disappearance on 3 December 1926 – or at least, in so far as she could recall them:

> The trouble really began with the death of my mother in the spring of 1926. That affected me very deeply, and on top of this shock there came a number of private troubles, into which I would rather not enter. Instead of sleeping well, as I had done previously, I began to suffer from insomnia, and slept on the average only two hours a night.[1]

The 'private troubles' referred to were undoubtedly a reference to her deteriorating relationship with Archie, which was also taking its toll on Agatha's health, both mentally and physically:

> I began to get confused and muddled over things. I never felt hungry and ate less and less. Sometimes I would sit down, put my hands to my head, and try to remember *what* it was I was doing. A terrible sense of loneliness was coming over me. I don't think I realised that for the first time in my life I was really ill. I had always been extremely strong, and I had no understanding of how unhappiness, worry and overwork could affect your physical health.[2]

That this was the case was confirmed by the *Harrogate Herald*, which reported on what it was told by Agatha's secretary, Carlo:

Miss [Charlotte] Fisher, Mrs Christie's secretary, says that she [Agatha] had not recovered from a serious breakdown earlier in the year. [This breakdown is alluded to by Agatha in her autobiography, where she described herself as being ill and unhappy.][3]

Agatha's interview with the *Daily Mail*, given on 16 February 1928, continued as follows:

Of course I know that at the time a large number of people thought that I had gone away to seek publicity, to carry out a stupid hoax, or to have a subtle revenge on somebody. What actually happened was this. On the day of my disappearance I drove over in the afternoon to Dorking with my daughter to see a relative. I was at this time in a very despondent state of mind. I just wanted my life to end. As I passed by Newlands Corner that afternoon I saw a quarry and there came into my mind the thought of driving into it. However, as my daughter [Rosalind] was with me in the car, I dismissed the idea at once.

That night I felt terribly miserable. I felt that I could go on no longer. I left home that night in a state of high nervous strain with the intention of doing something desperate. I left home at 10 o'clock in my car with a few articles of clothing in a suitcase and about £60 in my bag. I had drawn some money from the bank shortly before as I had decided to go that winter to South Africa with my daughter, and I wanted to make preparations.

All that night I drove aimlessly about. In my mind there was the vague idea of ending everything. I drove automatically down roads I knew, but without thinking where I was going. As far as I remember I went to London and drove to Euston Station. Why I went there I do not know. I believe I then drove out to Maidenhead, where I looked at the river. I thought about jumping in, but realised that I could swim too well to drown.

Agatha's novel *Unfinished Portrait,* has thus far provided a plausible and coherent account of Agatha's thoughts and emotions, even though she chose fictitious names for its characters and locations. Here, the story of the events leading up to Agatha's disappearance is told with a far greater candour than the more formal account given by Agatha in her autobiography. Here, Agatha's emotions are given unbridled expression.

In *Unfinished Portrait*, Agatha is 'Celia'; her husband Archie is 'Dermot'; her daughter Rosalind is 'Judy'; her dog Peter is 'Aubrey', and her secretary Miss Charlotte Fisher – (nicknamed Carlo) is 'Miss Hood'. As for

Archie's mistress Nancy Neele, she becomes 'Marjorie Connell'. If the novel is to be believed, then the events leading up to Agatha's and Archie's divorce were protracted.

One day, Celia (Agatha) notices that Miss Hood (Carlo) has a worried expression on her face, and she suspects the worst: Dermot has left home. This proves to be the case. However, Dermot returns, saying that he feels miserable, and that Celia had been correct when she told him that he should stay with herself and their daughter Judy. Dermot promises that he will try. However, it was her duty to get well again. Illness was something that he could not bear, nor unhappiness. Having confirmed that Dermot sincerely wishes to give their marriage another chance, Celia suggests that they remain together for 3 months, and at the end of that time, if Dermot feels unable to continue 'then that's that'. During this period, it is agreed that Dermot will not see his mistress Marjorie (Nancy Neele). Celia, however, is at the end of her tether. 'I'm afraid to go queer again…,' she says. (Is this an allusion by Agatha to the fact that she feels she may be losing her mind?)

Sadly, the plan does not work. Dermot not only continues to see Marjorie, but he goes on to ask Celia for a divorce. The narrative now moves on. It is late evening at Celia's family home (not Styles, but a cottage at Dalton Heath, 10 miles from Dermot's golf course), and Celia is about to disappear. Before doing so, she looks in at the nursery to check that Judy is sound asleep. Then, silently, she closes the door and goes downstairs to the front hall.

The similarity between this description and that given by Superintendent William Kenward to the Home Office is unmistakable. Having discovered that Agatha had left home late on the evening of 3 December 1926 'under rather unusual circumstances', the Superintendent also learned 'that Mrs Christie had been very depressed, and that just before leaving in the car, she had gone upstairs and kissed her little daughter (Rosalind), who was in bed asleep'.[4]

The novel continues with Celia's dog Aubrey, appearing in the hope that his mistress will take him for a walk. But Celia has other ideas. She cradles Aubrey's head between her hands, gives him a kiss on the nose, and then bids him goodbye, saying, 'Stay at home. Good dog'. She tells him he can't come with her, and that no one must accompany her to where she is going. She was exhausted after 'that long scene' with Dermot. Everything had become unbearable. She was desperate, and now she must escape.

The 'long scene' which Celia refers to, had occurred when Miss Hood was absent from the house – being away in London, where she was visiting a sister who had returned home from abroad. Dermot saw this as the ideal opportunity to get Celia on her own in order to 'have things out'. He now confessed, that despite his promise not to see Marjorie during that three month period, he had been unable to keep it. Celia, however, was by now past caring. All she wished, was for there to be no more of this verbal abuse from Dermot. She wished to hear no more of those 'cruel, hurting words', or to see 'those hostile, stranger's eyes…'.

For Celia (Agatha), there was now only one conclusion to be drawn. Although she loved her husband Dermot, he hated her, and this was more than she could bear. There was no alternative, but to take, 'the easiest way out…'. When he told her that he was going away for two days, she informed him that when he came back he would not find her there. Yes, of course she could go away, he said, but his expression revealed to her that he had understood her meaning all too well. But afterwards, of course, when it was 'all over', he would deny it, and try to convince everybody, himself included, that he had *not* understood her meaning. For him, this would be the easy way out of the situation.

This narrative appears to indicate that Agatha knew about the existence of Archie's mistress Nancy Neele. It also implies, that on the day of her disappearance, Archie and Agatha had a frank discussion, during the course of which the former admitted that he was still seeing Nancy Neele, even though he had promised not to. Agatha now hints to Archie that she intends to commit suicide (notwithstanding the fact that she has a daughter Rosalind), but Archie chooses to ignore this intimation.

Agatha, in her novel *Unfinished Portrait*, resumes the story. Celia had decided to go away – 'out of it all'. It had become too much for her to bear. The pain was too great. She had even gone past thinking of her daughter Judy. All that mattered now was her desire to escape. She had reached a bridge, beneath which was a swiftly running river. 'There was no one about…'.

Now, as Celia stands on the parapet, contemplating suicide, just as Agatha had done at Maidenhead, her mind turns to a former suitor of hers. Where was Peter Maitland (in real life, Agatha's former suitor Reggie Lucy)? She was aware that he had married after the war. She also knew that had *she* married him, he would have been kind to her, and that she would have been happy with him, happy and secure. Equally, she knew in her heart that she would never have loved him as she had loved Dermot. Dermot, who was 'so cruel…'.

In *Unfinished Portrait*, Agatha also revealed her mother Clara's ('Miriam's') early reservations about Archie. When she married him, said Miriam, she had not trusted him, believing him to be neither honest nor loyal. In fact, she went as far as to say she thought that he would have affairs with other women. And Celia had dismissed her mother's words with a laugh, telling her that Dermot never looked 'at anything but a golf ball!'

How these words, said presumably by Clara to Agatha, must have reverberated in the latter's mind at this point, as she regrets that she did not marry the 'kind' Peter Maitland when she had had the chance. 'The whole world was cruel, really – cruel and treacherous… The river was better…' Whereupon she clambered up, onto the parapet, and leapt off.

Unlike Celia, who leaps off the parapet into the river, Agatha herself decides that being a strong swimmer, death by drowning would be difficult to achieve. She, therefore, leaves the vicinity of Maidenhead, her subsequent movements being as follows:

I then drove back to London again, and then on to Sunningdale. From there I went to Newlands Corner. When I reached a point on the road which I thought was near the quarry I had seen in the afternoon, I turned the car off the road down the hill towards it. I left the [steering] wheel and let the car run. The car struck something with a jerk and pulled up suddenly. I was flung against the steering wheel, and my head hit something.

Up to this moment I was Mrs Christie. I was certainly in an abnormal state of mind, and scarcely knew what I was doing or where I was going. All the same I knew I was Mrs Christie. After the accident in the car, however, I lost my memory. For 24 hours after the accident my mind was an almost complete blank. Since I recovered my health I have managed to recall a little of what happened in those 24 hours.

In her somewhat rambling and disjointed account to the *Daily Mail*, Agatha also mentions injuring her chest and her head in the crash, being 'dazed by the blow', and wandering 'in a dream' for 24 hours:

I remember arriving at a big railway station and asking what it was and being surprised to learn it was Waterloo. It is strange that the railway authorities there did not recall me, as I was covered with mud and I had smeared blood on my face from a cut in my hand. I could never make out how this cut had been caused. I believe I wandered about London and I then remember arriving at the hotel in Harrogate. I was still muddy and showing signs of the accident when I arrived there.

The circumstances of Agatha's flight will now be discussed in more detail.

From Styles to Harrogate, a
Reconstruction of the Journey

From her house Styles at Sunningdale, Berkshire, Agatha describes driving 'aimlessly about': first to London, then to Maidenhead, and then returning home, before finally arriving at Newlands Corner in the neighbouring county of Surrey. The total distance involved for these journeys is approximately 175 miles. Assuming an average speed of 25–30mph, this would have taken Agatha at least 7 hours. Adding one hour for stops, this suggests that (having left home at 10p.m.) she arrived at Newlands Corner at about 6a.m. on the morning of Saturday 4 December. So does this fit in with the known facts?

According to Superintendent Kenward's statement to the Home Office, Edward McAlister told him that it was 6.20a.m. when he helped Agatha to start her vehicle. This correlates well with Agatha's own account of her movements, which, as indicated above, would appear to suggest that she arrived at Newlands Corner at about 6a.m.

However, McAlister's observation that Agatha's hair was covered with hoar-frost, and that the car radiator was 'quite cold' (a somewhat ambiguous choice of words) is puzzling, because it implies that the car had been stationary for some time before he arrived on the scene, with Agatha either standing outside it, or sitting in it with its retractable hood in the 'down' position. This latter proposition is not so far fetched as it may seem, because, as will be demonstrated shortly, Agatha was not in her right mind at the time.

From Agatha's own account, and from the description of the car when found, it is difficult to escape the conclusion, that after McAlister had restarted her car, she drove off towards Clandon before returning to Newlands Corner where she made a genuine attempt at suicide, presumably by attempting to drive over the edge of the quarry. What state of mind must she have been in to put at risk her beloved Morris Cowley (a vehicle which was her pride and joy), let alone her own life? Her attempt having failed, she now decided to abandon the car.

According to McAlister, Agatha's car was discovered about two hours after his early-morning encounter with her – i.e. at about 8.20a.m. According to Frederick Dore, who made the discovery, the vehicle's lights were off, having 'evidently been left on until the current became exhausted'. This conflicts with Superintendent Kenward's statement to the Home Office in which he says, 'I subsequently found that the car headlights were still burning early on the morning of the 4th [December 1926]'.[1]

Clearly, Agatha could not have been expected to embark on foot, carrying all the items which were subsequently discovered to have been left behind by her in the car. They included, 'a Fur Coat, a Dressing Case containing various articles of ladies' wearing apparel, and a driving licence indicating that the owner was Mrs Agatha Christie of Sunningdale, Berks'.[2] But why, on a cold and frosty winter's night, did she opt to leave her fur coat behind? Also, why were these items strewn about? Was this the result of her scrabbling about in the darkness looking for something, possibly her purse? Or could it be that after the crash, Agatha did not recognize the items as her own, even though they were? Perhaps she may even not have recognized the car itself as being her own. Fanciful – even absurd – as these ideas may appear at first sight, nevertheless, they are distinct possibilities, as will shortly be demonstrated.

How had the journey from Newlands Corner to London's Waterloo train station been accomplished? The assumption must be that Agatha, having composed herself after the crash, walked back to the main road and on to Clandon train station (a distance of 3 miles) on Southern Railways' Guildford to London line. (Alternatively, she may have caught the train at Guildford, 4 miles away). According to the timetable, there were two or three trains every hour from Guildford to London (a 30 mile, one-hour journey); the first one that morning departing at 5.42a.m. The likelihood is, therefore, that Agatha commenced her train journey sometime around 8a.m., and arrived in London at about 9a.m.

Having alighted from the train, Agatha, in her own words, 'wandered about London...'. So where did she go? There is circumstantial evidence that she visited the city's south-west district, because the letter dated

4 December, which she sent to her husband Archie's younger brother Captain Campbell Christie (whom she described as 'a great friend and… a kind and lovable person'[3]), was postmarked 'London SW'. The letter was franked at 9.45 (a.m.), which means that Agatha must have posted it shortly before this time (otherwise it would have been taken with an earlier collection). This is just feasible in the light of what is known about Agatha's movements. Why did she choose to send the letter to Campbell's workplace, the Royal Military Academy, Woolwich, instead of to his home address, also at Woolwich? This may simply have been because she did not have his home address with her at the time, but remembered where he worked.

Agatha made her way across London to King's Cross train station (probably by taxi), where she caught the London and North Eastern Railway (LNER) train to the north. According to the LNER timetable for that day, there was a through-train, scheduled to leave King's Cross at 1.40p.m. and arrive at Harrogate at 6.10p.m. This correlates with police reports, indicating that Agatha arrived by taxi at the Harrogate Hydropathic Hotel – 'The Hydro' – shortly before 7p.m.

Agatha Transformed

Now, at the reuniting of Agatha and Archie on the evening of 14 December 1926 at the Harrogate Hydro, the *Harrogate Advertiser* reported upon what was perhaps the most extraordinary phenomenon of all:

> He [Archie] went up and spoke to her [Agatha], but she did not recognise him as her husband. She turned to some fellow guests and said, 'I am excited because my brother has arrived.'[1]

And the *Daily Mail* in its report confirmed that Agatha believed Archie to be her brother:

> It is stated that after dinner she [Agatha] introduced the colonel [Archie] to a visitor as her brother. She has always taken a morning and evening paper. Tonight she read a paper in which was the headline, 'Mrs Christie, the novelist, said to be in a Harrogate hydro.' I am told that it did not appear to convey anything to her. Col. and Mrs Christie have tonight, I understand, engaged a small, private suite [at The Hydro]. They are expected to leave The Hydro early tomorrow to go south.[2]

This provides further proof that Agatha had completely lost her sense of identity. In a sense, this was a critical moment in Agatha's life. It represented an earthquake following a collision in her mind of two tectonic plates: her hopes and dreams on the one hand, and harsh reality on the other.

To Archie, the realization that his wife did not recognize him, her husband of fourteen years, would have come as a great shock, although it would be idle to pretend that he was still in any way in love with her by that time; for by now his attentions were firmly fixed on his mistress Nancy Neele. The seasoned police officer Superintendent McDowell, who was also a witness to the event, would in all probability have been equally astonished. Could Agatha have been bluffing? Was this some weird device by which she meant to punish Archie, her errant husband? From Archie's subsequent remarks, and he was someone who knew Agatha better than most, this was definitely not the case, and it is to Archie's credit that he did not attempt to discredit Agatha by pretending otherwise.

Archie did not know it at the time, but would discover all too soon, that this was only part of the story; for it transpired that from the time Agatha had arrived at The Hydro, she had behaved in a most extraordinary manner. Said the *Harrogate Advertiser*:

> The lady in question arrived at the Harrogate Hydro on Saturday night, December 4th, and had with her only an attaché case. She registered under the name of Mrs Teresa Neele, and was understood to have come from the Cape Colony.

This is borne out by the *Harrogate Herald* of 15 December 1926, which printed a comprehensive list of guests staying at various hotels in the town, including 'HARROGATE HYDRO', where Agatha's presence is signified by the simple entry 'Neele, Mrs, Cape Town':

> There was nothing unusual about her appearance to lead the manager to suspect she was the missing novelist... During her stay she acted as an ordinary guest and took part in the dancing and singing at the Sunday evening concert. She even tried to dance the Charleston with an elderly partner, but did not appear to know the steps. She conversed freely with the other guests and gave them to understand she had been in Torquay... She talked in a perfectly rational manner and nothing in her speech or manner aroused any suspicion. She visited places of entertainment with friends she made in the hotel, and took walks round the town. It is stated that she purchased many books of detective fiction, and that she was a great reader of the newspapers. At first, it was thought that she was reading about her own disappearance, but her chief interest was in crossword puzzles.[3]

On Saturday 11 December 1926, an advertisement appeared in *The Times* newspaper, which reinforces the idea that Agatha was suffering from some sort of identity crisis; one which involved not only herself, but also her family and friends. The advertisement, as was subsequently discovered, was placed there by Agatha herself:

FRIENDS and RELATIVES of TERESA NEELE, late of South Africa, COMMUNICATE. Write Box R.702, The Times, E.C.4.

Archie's explanation for this was as follows:

> She thought the relatives and family must know where she was [i.e. at The Hydro], although she could not remember who they were. At last, hearing nothing of them, she became worried and advertised asking them to communicate with her.[4]

As already stated, throughout her childhood Agatha had suffered from recurrent night terrors, in which a sinister figure whom she called The Gunman threatened to take the place of one, or more of the people who were nearest and dearest to her. It is, therefore, ironic that now, it seemed, she herself had become the victim of such a 'take over', in that her mind appeared to be possessed by another person.

On 15 December 1926, the *Daily Mail*'s Special Correspondent gave further details of Agatha's time at the Hydro:

> ...it is understood, she has bought a good many clothes since she has been here. She has worn evening clothes every night at dinner with a fancy scarf round her shoulders. For the first few days she spoke to scarcely anybody, but since then she has made a number of friends. On one occasion she has played billiards, but her playing is indifferent and she has rarely made more than five or six [points] at a time. She has not gone out very much, but had read almost constantly, having a book with her at her meals. On only one occasion has she breakfasted in the dining-room. On other days she has breakfasted in her room, but she has always appeared for luncheon and has eaten heartily.[5]

Agatha's account of events, given over a year later to the *Daily Mail* newspaper, confirms that she did indeed experience a change of identity, for as she herself stated, up to the moment of the car crash, 'I was Mrs Christie,' whereas on her arrival at the Harrogate Hydro, 'I had now become in my mind Mrs Teresa Neele of South Africa.'

> I can quite understand why I went to Harrogate. The motor-car accident brought on neuritis, and once before in my life I had thought of going to Harrogate to have treatment for this complaint. While I was in Harrogate I had treatment regularly.

This correlates with the fact that in Agatha's hotel room at The Hydro, the police discovered a bottle of laudanum, an opiate-based analgesic used in the treatment of neuritis. This had been prescribed for her by a Torquay pharmacist, indicating, that as she said, she had been suffering from this complaint even before the car crash, which appears to have exacerbated it. Agatha continued:

> The only thing which really puzzled me was the fact that I had scarcely any luggage with me. I could not quite make this out. I had not even a toothbrush in my case, and I wondered why I had come there without one. I realised, of course, that I had been in some kind of accident. I had a severe bruise on my chest, and my head was also bruised. As Mrs Neele I was very happy and contented. I had become, as it were, a new woman, and all the worries and anxieties of Mrs Christie had left me.
>
> At Harrogate I read every day about Mrs Christie's disappearance, and came to the conclusion that she was dead. I regarded her as having acted stupidly. I was greatly struck by my resemblance to her and pointed it out to other people in the hotel. It never occurred to me that I might be her, as I was quite satisfied in my mind as to who I was. I thought I was a widow, and that I had had a son who had died, for I had in my bag a photograph of my little girl when very young with the name 'Teddy' upon it. I even tried to obtain a book by this Mrs Christie to read.[6]

From Agatha's story, as recounted by the *Daily Mail*, it appears that up to the time of the car crash she was quite sure about her identity; whereas by the time she arrived at the Harrogate Hydropathic Hotel some fourteen hours later, she was convinced that she was another person. And in her new identity, Agatha recognized neither her former self, Agatha Christie (even when she saw her own photograph in the newspapers of the day, which were reporting on the continuing search for her), nor her daughter Rosalind (whose photograph she carried with her and whom she mistook for a son), nor her family or friends. How could this alteration in Agatha's mind have occurred? After all, there was nothing in her past to indicate that she was in any way mentally deranged.

Agatha having been reunited with Archie at The Hydro, the *Harrogate Herald* resumes the story:

> Immediately afterwards the two went into the dining-room for dinner. Col. and Mrs Christie stayed the night [of 14 December] at the Hydro. Mrs Christie was attired in salmon pink nulon [brand name for material made of synthetic fibre]. Col. Christie said there was no question of her identity. 'She is my wife. She is suffering from complete loss of memory and identity. She does not know who she is. We are hoping to take her to London to-morrow to see doctors and specialists and we hope with rest and quiet that she will be fully restored.'[7]

The *Harrogate Advertiser* reported that 'During the morning [of Wednesday 15 December] Mrs Christie's sister [Madge] and her brother-in-law [James Watts] arrived at The Hydro, but did not go away with them [i.e. with the Christies].' Although in his statement to the *Harrogate Herald* Archie had mentioned London as being their destination, this was a subtle ploy to mislead the press. In fact, Agatha and Archie 'left by the 9.35 train for Manchester',[8] en route to Abney Hall, the Watts's family home, at Cheadle near Manchester.

On 16 December 1926, Archie elaborated on Agatha's condition:

> My wife is extremely ill, suffering from complete loss of memory. Three years have dropped out of her life. She cannot recall anything that has happened during that period. The fact that she lives at Sunningdale has no significance for her, and she does not seem to realize that her home is at The Styles [usually referred to simply as Styles]. As to what has happened since she left there, her mind is a complete blank. She has not the slightest recollection of going to Newlands Corner, or proceeding, eventually, to Harrogate. As was only to be expected, she is very much upset, as the result of the journey yesterday [from Harrogate to Abney Hall], and has no idea what all the fuss is about. She now knows who I am, and has also realized that Mrs Watts is her sister.

This latter development was a step forward, and must have been a further relief to those around Agatha. However, her recovery was far from complete, as Archie's statement confirms:

> It is somewhat remarkable that she does not know she has a daughter. In this connexion, when she was shown a picture of herself and Rosalind, her little daughter, she asked who the child was, 'What is the child like?' And, 'How old is she?'[9]

Faced with this situation, it was clear both to Archie and to the Watts family that the only possibility of resolving the situation was, immediately, to seek expert professional help, which is what they did. Said Archie on Thursday 16 December 1926:

> My wife has been seen today by a local doctor, and this afternoon a specialist is coming over from Manchester for a further consultation.[10]

That same day, Madge's family doctor Henry Wilson, and Donald Core MD, a specialist in nervous disorders from Manchester, issued the following statement:

> After careful examination of Mrs Agatha Christie this afternoon, we have formed the opinion that she is suffering from an unquestionably genuine loss of memory and that for her future welfare she should be spared all further anxiety and excitement.[11]

The doctors also recommended that Agatha consult a psychiatrist.

On 17 December 1926, Archie left Abney Hall and returned to London. Daughter Rosalind was now brought from Sunningdale to be with her mother. On 15 January, Agatha (with Rosalind and Carlo) transferred to a flat in Kensington. She now commenced a course of therapy under a Harley Street psychiatrist (of unknown name) who said of his last meeting with Agatha:

> This was the final session of Mrs Christie's programme of the hypnosis technique by mutual agreement. For my part in the course of treatment I have been completely convinced by the authenticity of her condition. Despite the ingenuity of Mrs Christie's mind I can find no evidence of

fakery. I believe that there was a mental stimulus to this hiatus of hers. And there was a motivation: in her confused state she exacted a kind of rough justice [i.e. on her erring husband, Archie] which her normal mind would not sanction.[12]

So much for the present. As for the future, as will be seen; it would be a considerable number of years before psychiatry would become sufficiently advanced to enable an adequate diagnosis of Agatha's symptoms to be made. In the meantime, the question was, would Agatha make a full recovery and regain her former mental faculties?

The Mystery Solved?

In order to make sense of Agatha's strange behaviour following her car crash of 4 December 1926, the first question to be asked is, was it brought about by the consequent blow to the head, which by her own account, she undoubtedly sustained? To quote from *Clinical Medicine: A Textbook for Medical Students and Doctors*:

> In a mild [head] injury a patient is first stunned or dazed for a few seconds or minutes. Loss of consciousness is transient and following this the patient is alert and there is no amnesia [loss of memory].[1]

In Agatha's case, she admits to being dazed, but there appears to have been no loss of consciousness. The *Oxford Handbook of Psychiatry*, however, under the heading, 'Psychiatric aspects of head injury', describes a condition called 'Post-traumatic syndrome' (also called 'post-concussional syndrome'):

> This is a common phenomenon after head injury. The main symptoms are: headache; dizziness; insomnia; irritability; emotional lability; increased sensitivity to noise, light, etc; fatigue; poor concentration; anxiety; and depression.[2]

This in no way resembles the picture painted of Agatha at the Harrogate Hydro, where she blended into her surroundings, read the newspapers, visited the shops and so forth. This opinion is shared by psychoanalyst Darian Leader:

It seems that there is very little evidence that it was amnesia. She [Agatha] did not approach anyone to find out something about her identity, as amnesics often do. She did not approach a policeman or someone in uniform, something that happens commonly in amnesia and the kind of behaviour that one might expect from an amnesic patient. [He therefore concludes that] On the contrary, it seems much more probable that she [Agatha] was in a trance-like state.[3]

Agreed. So will the mindset of Agatha following her car crash remain a mystery for all time? The answer is no, because another source, the *Oxford Textbook of Psychiatry*, contains a description of another syndrome which, it seems, fits her like the proverbial glove:

Psychogenic amnesia starts suddenly. Patients are unable to recall long periods of their lives and sometimes deny any knowledge of their previous life or personal identity. In psychogenic fugue [in which a person loses the awareness of their own identity] the patient not only loses his [or her] memory but also wanders away from his usual surrounding. When found he usually denies all memory of his whereabouts during the period of wandering, and may also deny knowledge of his personal identity. Fugues also occur in epilepsy, severe depressive disorders [as with Agatha], and alcoholism. They may also be associated with suicide attempts [again, as with Agatha]. Many patients who present in fugue give a history of seriously disturbed relationships with their parents in childhood, and many others are habitual liars.[4] [It should be emphasized that there is no suggestion that this latter characteristic in any way applies to Agatha.]

For those who are unfamiliar with the more bizarre workings of the human mind, the notion that Agatha may have been suffering from psychogenic amnesia may come as something of a shock. The condition, however, is nowadays accepted as a definite clinical syndrome, and there are many descriptions of it in the literature. Researcher Georgia Griffin, for example, sheds further light on the subject:

Eyewitnesses report that someone in the midst of a dissociative [i.e. psychogenic] fugue appears to behave normally, 'apart from [an] inability to recall their past or personal information.' However, when a fuguer 'comes to' she often behaves as though she has just been awoken from a deep sleep, that is, she appears dazed and disorientated. In addition, such an individual is unable to recall how she arrived at her destination, or why. Not surprisingly, the brain activity of someone in the midst of a dissociative disorder like fugue [as measured by an electroencephalogram] is slightly slower than in normal awake activity.[5] [In other words, the state of fugue has a definite organic basis.]

Finally, *The Oxford Companion to the Mind* confirms what probably precipitated the fugue in which Agatha found herself:

The individual who enters into a fugue state is sometimes escaping from an intolerable situation or suffering from a severe depression. This wandering behaviour has been equated with an act of suicide, with the patient seeking some state of nirvana which will free him [or in this case her] from his worldly cares and responsibilities.[6]

Unfinished Portrait

As is so often the case, Agatha's novel contains a vital piece of information, because 'Celia' (the thinly disguised Agatha) actually describes going into a fugue state when (as Agatha herself did) she leaves home in desperation. She then not only forgets her late mother's name, but also her own identity.

Celia walked on and on, through the rain and the wet, but was unable to remember the purpose of the walk. Then, suddenly, realized she was going to the police station, but where was it? 'Surely, in a town, not out in the open country', which was where she was presently heading. She turned around and walked the other way. She knew the police would help her, once she had given them her mother's name. But what was it? She could not remember. In fact, she could not even remember her own name, which she found frightening. Celia then goes on to echo Agatha's own suicidal feelings. She stumbled over a ditch, which she noticed was full of water. How easy it would be to drown oneself in water – a much preferable end than attempting to hang oneself. One simply had to lie down in the water...

Only with the knowledge of what a psychogenic fugue state is, is it possible, satisfactorily, to interpret Agatha's mindset and behaviour following the car crash, and also to provide an explanation for some of the questions that have remained unanswered for so many decades. As a result, some of the conclusions now reached may be seen as startling, when viewed from the perspective of the so-called 'normal' mind.

From Agatha's Perspective

Agatha's thoughts and actions from the time of the car crash on 4 December 1926, will now be described from her point of view on the one hand (the author hopefully echoing her thoughts accurately), and from the known facts on the other. In this there is, clearly, a degree of speculation, as there were no witnesses to some of the events described. Therefore, the reader must be left to judge for him or herself, the plausibility of the explanation offered.

Agatha is believed to have entered into the fugue state, either gradually or suddenly, at some time between the car crash and her arrival at The Hydro in Harrogate, at which point she said she had become, in her mind, Mrs Teresa Neele.

After the car crash, Agatha has entered, probably only partially, into the fugue state. She does not recognize the car, her beloved Morris Cowley, as her own; nor the items in it. This is why, on a bitterly cold winter's night, she not only abandons the car, but also many of her personal effects including a fur coat – hers, but not recognized as such – which could have kept her warm.

She now makes her way back up the slope towards the main road. For some reason the name 'Harrogate' comes into her mind. For some time she has been considering a visit to that spa town in Yorkshire, which had become a Mecca for those seeking to be healed of rheumatic and similar diseases. (This is on account of the town's Royal Baths,[7] with their medicinal and healing properties, which were opened by the Duke of Clarence in 1897).

Agatha has sufficient memory to recall that there is a railway station at nearby Clandon, so she makes her way on foot towards it. From here, she embarks on a train that will take her there, via London.

Equally, having arrived in the capital, she has the presence of mind to write a letter to her brother-in-law Campbell Christie, and also to know that to get to Harrogate she must cross the city and catch the train from King's Cross Station – which she does. At Harrogate, she is still *compos mentis* enough to realize that it is that town's Hydropathic Hotel – The Hydro – which is her destination. However, when she arrives there on the evening of Saturday 4 December, the fugue state has taken over completely, and she now believes that she is Mrs Teresa Neele from Cape Town.

Why 'Teresa Neele' and why 'Cape Town'? Perhaps these names were dredged up from her subconscious mind. Agatha later revealed that she adopted the name Teresa because of an acquaintance of hers of that name who lived in Torquay.[7] Neele, on the other hand, was the surname of Archie's mistress Nancy. Could her choice of this particular name, above all others, have been a subconscious attempt by Agatha to assume the identity of the object of Archie's affection – i.e. his mistress, and thereby win him back? As for Cape Town, this was a place which she had already visited on the world tour with Archie and Major Belcher in 1922, and she was currently in the process of making arrangements to visit there again that winter for a holiday, in company with her daughter Rosalind.

Or if it was not her subconscious mind which had led her to make these selections, then could it have been something that she was carrying on her person – perhaps a letter, a postcard, travel tickets, that reminded her of these people and places, and therefore led her to make these false assumptions?

Having arrived at The Hydro, Agatha's memory finally deserts her completely. From now on, it is only the 'here and now' that impinges itself upon her altered consciousness.

Agatha, who was observed to be a regular reader of the newspaper, sees not only the press reports of her disappearance, but also several photographs of herself, which she does not recognize. In discussion with other guests, she speaks of Agatha Christie as if she is another person. Nevertheless, she retains the capacity to enjoy reading the newspapers, and even to do their crosswords, as well as to dance and play the piano.

Agatha cannot understand why, since her arrival, no family or friends have contacted her. She therefore places an advertisement in *The Times* newspaper, in the hope that someone will come forward.

However, as she persists in using the name 'Teresa Neele', it is not surprising that she receives no response. Eleven days after her disappearance, Agatha, at last, has a visit from a member of her family. Her brother has arrived.

In fact, the person who has arrived at The Hydro is not her brother Monty, as she believes, but her husband Archie, whom, in her fugue state, she fails to recognize. When Archie declared, shortly afterwards, that Agatha now knew who he was, and also who her sister Madge and Madge's husband James Watts (who by now were also on the scene) were, this remains doubtful. Archie had no medical knowledge, and it may be that Agatha simply 'knew' who they were because of what they told her. For Agatha, coming out of the fugue state would be a long and gradual process, and gaps would remain in her memory, even after many years.

Conclusion

Although Agatha may have been temporarily dazed by her car crash, it does not explain her subsequent behaviour. Instead, the symptoms of 'psychogenic amnesia and fugue state', as described above, would appear to fit her condition perfectly. In the light of present knowledge, those members of the press and the medical profession who wrote of Agatha at the time may be forgiven for not being able, fully, to comprehend it. Others, however, who have sought in more recent times to ascribe to Agatha some ulterior or even sinister motive, may not.

As indicated above, to a person experiencing a psychogenic fugue state and consequent loss of memory, the 'here and now' is all important. Confronted with images from the past, they are obliged to make sense of them in their own way, without the benefit of background knowledge, as Agatha did when shown a photograph of her daughter Rosalind, believing it to be that of her son (who in fact did not exist), or, when she was confronted by Archie, believing him to be her brother.

Even later, when the psychiatrist whom Agatha consulted, showed her some of her own make-up apparel, she failed to recognize these items, indicating that she was still, to some extent, in the fugue state.[8] A recognition that she was in this state of fugue is fundamental to understanding Agatha's behaviour, following her flight from home on the night of 3 December 1926.

Those who remain sceptical, despite all the evidence, and persist in believing that Agatha, in her disappearance, was acting out some kind of elaborate charade, should ask themselves, is it really conceivable that this lady (admittedly, the supreme contriver of plots) was able to hoodwink her friends and family, not to mention a family medical practitioner, a consultant in nervous diseases, and a Harley Street psychiatrist? And if this had been the case, why did she feel it necessary, years later, to consult the Regius Professor of Pastoral Theology at Oxford, described as 'a well-known psychoanalyst', who she hoped (in vain as it transpired) would enable her to fill in the gaps which still persisted in her memory?[9]

25

Divorce

In January 1927 (5 weeks after her disappearance), Agatha took her daughter Rosalind and Carlo for a holiday to the Canary Islands. On her return, she moved into a small flat in Chelsea. This part of Agatha's life is once again paralleled by her in *Unfinished Portrait*, where Celia [Agatha], having become unwell, goes to Switzerland to recuperate.

Finally, having regained her health and strength, Celia returned to England, where she wrote to Dermot, telling him that she did not believe in divorce. In fact, what she did believe in was the old fashioned concept of a couple sticking together, and enduring whatever unpleasantness may come along, for the sake of the children. She realized that he probably did not agree with her in this, and she had often heard people say that it was better for the children's sake, if parents who did not get on together went their separate ways. She told him that to her way of thinking, the notion that squabbling parents should part for the good of the children, was an invalid one. This was because a child's need for both parents was paramount, however much the parents might be quarrelling. This was what life was like.

As far as her own parents were concerned, Agatha declared that her home had been 'too happy', and she had, therefore, grown up as 'a fool...'. In other words, she had been brought up in an altogether too cloistered and artificial environment. It must be said, that in expressing these thoughts, Agatha was speaking theoretically, in the sense that she had no first-hand experience of being brought up in a home where the parents were in conflict – quite the reverse, in fact. Had it been otherwise, and had she realized the destructive effect of a bad home atmosphere on a child in its formative years, she might well have thought differently.

As for the sentiments expressed latterly, yes, her cosy and over-protected upbringing had left her entirely unprepared for life in the raw, and also with an abiding shyness, which she would probably have easily overcome had she been permitted as a child, to mingle more with her peers.

Celia told her husband Dermot, that in her opinion, a love affair was of little significance, and that he could be perfectly free, just so long as he treated Judy with kindness, and behaved like a good father to her. In her heart, Celia knew that Dermot meant more to her daughter than she could ever mean, and that the only reason Judy ever wanted her mother was for physical comfort when she was ill. Otherwise, in Judy's mind, it was she and her father who belonged together. Celia promised Dermot that if he returned she would not scold him or rebuke him, and that in view of the suffering which they had both endured, she would like them to treat each other with kindness. The choice was his. But he must realize that she neither believed in, nor desired a divorce, and that if he chose to go down that path, then the responsibility rested with him alone.

In the event, Celia's efforts were to no avail, because Dermot's response was to send her fresh evidence of his adultery with his mistress. She now had no choice but to divorce him, even though the court proceedings – having to be cross-examined and answer intimate questions – were hateful to her. In fact, they made her feel sick. Celia reflected, that had she given in at the beginning, and allowed Dermot to have his way, she would have saved herself 'a lot of pain and horror…'. Did she feel gratified that she had not given in earlier? She simply did not know. Neither did she know *why* she gave in. It might have been simply that she was 'tired and wanted peace', or that she felt it was the only thing to do. Perhaps, in her heart of hearts, she actually *wanted* to give in to Dermot? And now that she *had* given in, she was left with the feeling that she had betrayed Judy in favour of Dermot, and this is why now, every time her daughter looked at her, she felt guilty.

Celia's guilt feelings are based on the notion that a couple should remain together no matter what. In recent times, however, it is recognized that this may not always be the best way forward, nor may it be in the best interests of the child.

In April 1928, Agatha and Archie were granted a decree nisi, and on 29 October of that year, the couple's divorce was finalized. On 16 November, Archie married Nancy Neele. Agatha was later to make some poignant allusions to the breakdown of her marriage. She spoke of loyalty as the quality which she admired above all others. Loyalty and courage were, in her opinion, two of the most admirable virtues. Of Archie's courage, there was no doubt. He had proved this, time and again, during his service in the First World War. As for loyalty: this was an ingredient which, on his part, was lacking, as far as his marriage to Agatha was concerned. 'I realized, as I suppose many women realize, sooner or later, that the only person who can really hurt you in life is a husband,' said Agatha, bitterly.

There is no doubt that the family's wire-haired terrier Peter played a significant part in sustaining Agatha in her troubles. She would later describe herself as going through a very hard time (i.e. her divorce) with nothing but a dog to cling to.[2] It is no coincidence that Agatha dedicated *Dumb Witness*, published in 1937, to Peter, who was 'the most faithful of friends and dearest of companions, a dog in a thousand'.

26

Recovery

Said Agatha:

When I was finally discovered [i.e. at Harrogate following the motor car crash of the night of 3/4 December 1926] it was not for some time that doctors and relatives restored in my mind, memories of my life as Mrs Christie. These memories were drawn from my subconscious mind slowly. First I recalled my childhood days and thought of relatives and friends as they were when children. By gradual steps, I recalled later and later episodes in my life until I could remember what happened just before the motor accident. The doctors even made me try to recall the events in the blank 24 hours afterwards, as they said that for the health of my mind there should be no hiatus of any kind in my recollections. That is why I can now recall at the same time my existence as Mrs Christie and Mrs Neele.

When I was brought back to my life as Mrs Christie, again, many of my worries and anxieties returned, and although I am now quite well and cheerful and have lost my old morbid tendencies completely I have not quite that utter happiness of Mrs Neele.[1]

(She recorded this account in February 1928, a little over two years after the date of her disappearance).

As already stated, it is highly probable that in her novel *Unfinished Portrait*, Agatha (through her character Celia) is reflecting her own feelings at the time of her divorce. So does the story also give any clue as to the progress of her recovery, following her presumed attempt at suicide in the car crash (although, unlike Agatha, Celia attempted to kill herself by jumping off a parapet into a river)?

Larraby, the former portrait painter whom Celia met on the island, took her under his wing, so to speak. When she confided in him that she had been too happy as a child, he concurred, saying that one is never prepared when one is a child, for the things which might happen in the future. He, himself, had felt like she feels now: that life was not worth living. He had known 'that blinding despair', where it is only possible to 'see one way out'. However, he could reassure Celia that it would pass; that grief would not last forever, and that one day time would console and heal, given the chance. To this, Celia tells him that she knows exactly what he means. She *had* felt like that (i.e. suicidal). In fact, she had 'one try' which 'didn't come off', and subsequently she was glad that it had not.[2]

The words, 'I had one try' from Celia, are highly significant because they imply without any ambiguity, that Agatha's car crash on 3 December 1926, was in fact a deliberate attempt on her part to commit suicide.

Celia was now aged thirty-nine; a strong and healthy person who envisaged living, at least to the age of seventy, and perhaps beyond. The problem was, that she could not countenance the prospect of another thirty-five empty years of living alone. Larraby took a more optimistic view. She was wrong; the years would not be empty. 'Something will bloom again to fill them,' he said. Celia was not in the least reassured by his words, maintaining that the future was something that she simply could not face. When Larraby accused her of being a coward on this account, she readily acquiesced. 'I've always been a coward,' she said, and thought it strange that other people had not seen it as clearly as she had. Yes, she confessed that she was afraid...[3]

How did Agatha feel about men after this? Again, the answer is to be found in *Unfinished Portrait*, where Celia has this to say. Thoughtless people had told her that one day she would get married again, to some kind man who would put everything right for her. But this could never be. She would be too terrified to marry. 'Nobody can hurt you except a husband – nobody's near enough.'[4] But finally, she relents and accepts a proposal from a man called Michael. However, on the day before the wedding, the nightmare returns and she now imagines him (Michael) to be '*The Gun Man all over again...*', intruding upon her happy and contented life, and bringing back once more, a feeling of terror. She simply could not face repeating the experience: the fear and the knowledge that she could never trust anyone again – not even Michael. It would be hell for whoever it happened to be, just as it would be for her.[5]

1. *The Mysterious Affair at Styles* (Agatha's first published novel, where Hercule Poirot and Captain Hastings make their debut), London: The Bodley Head (1920).

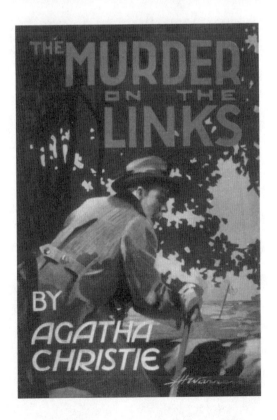

2. *The Murder on the Links*, London: The Bodley Head (1923).

3. *The Man in the Brown Suit*, London: The Bodley Head (1924).

4. *Poirot Investigates*, London: The Bodley Head (1924).

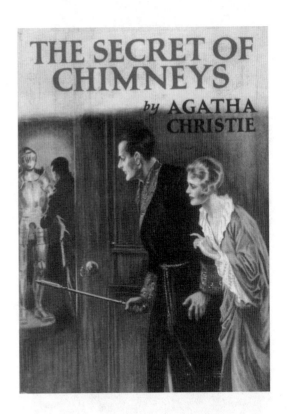

5. *The Secret of Chimneys*, London: The
Bodley Head (1925).

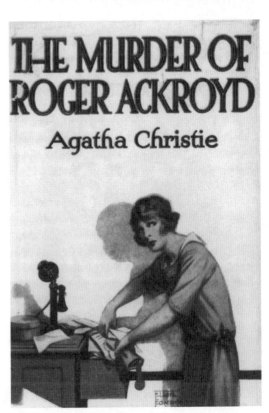

6. *The Murder of Roger Ackroyd*, London:
Collins (1926).

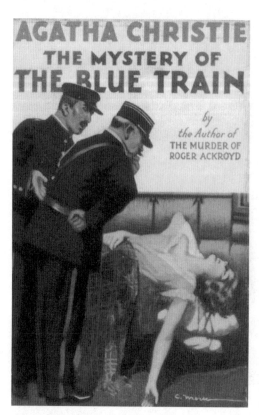

7. *The Mystery of the Blue Train*, London: Collins (1928).

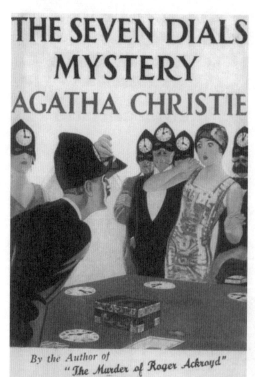

8. *The Seven Dials Mystery*, London: Collins (1929).

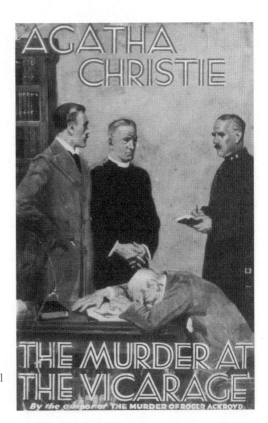

9. *The Murder at the Vicarage* (the first novel to feature Miss Jane Marple), London: Collins, The Crime Club (1930).

10. *The Sittaford Mystery*, London: Collins, The Crime Club (1931).

11. *Peril at End House*, London: Collins, The Crime Club (1932).

12. *The Hound of Death*, London: Odhams Press (1933).

13. *Lord Edgware Dies*, London: Collins, The Crime Club (1933).

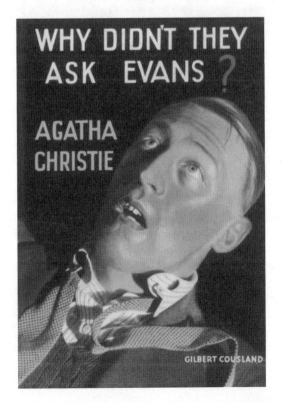

14. *Why didn't they ask Evans?* London: Collins, The Crime Club (1934).

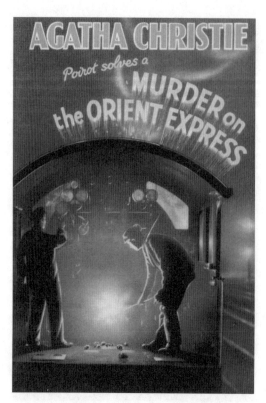

15. *Murder on the Orient Express*, London: Collins, The Crime Club (1934).

16. *Death in the Clouds*, London: Collins, The Crime Club (1935).

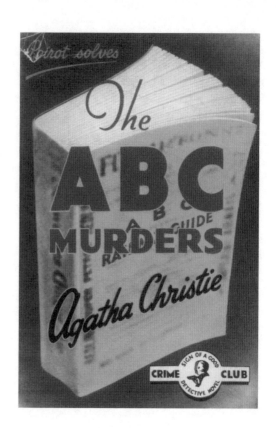

17. *The ABC Murders*, London: Collins, The Crime Club (1936).

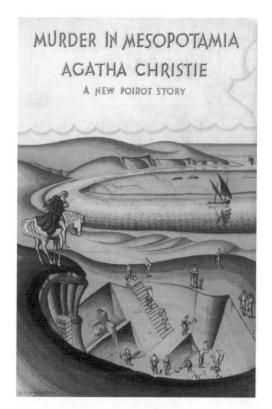

18. *Murder in Mesopotamia*, London: Collins, The Crime Club (1936).

19. *Dumb Witness*, London: Collins, The Crime Club (1937).

20. *Death on the Nile*, London: Collins, The Crime Club (1937).

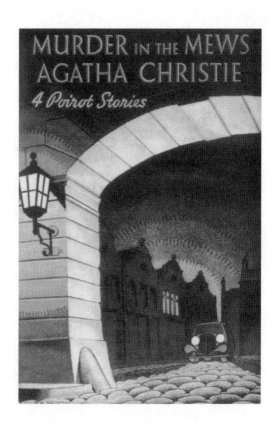

21. *Murder in the Mews*, London: Collins,
The Crime Club (1936).

22. *Hercule Poirot's Christmas*, London:
Collins, The Crime Club (1939).

23. *One, Two Buckle my Shoe*, London: Collins, The Crime Club (1940).

24. *The Body in the Library*, London: Collins, The Crime Club (1942).

Right: 25. 4.50 from Paddington.

Below: 26. Map of Harrogate.

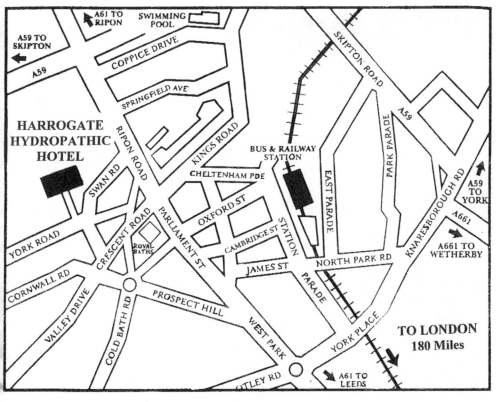

SUMMARY TABLES
THESE TABLES SHOW THE TRAIN SERVICES BY ALL ROUTES
In some cases alternative higher fares are in operation by routes other than the shortest

LONDON TABLES

LONDON (King's Cross) and BEN RHYDDING, ILKLEY, HARROGATE and RIPON.

											WEEKDAYS (exc Saturdays)									SUNDAYS			
		H	DR	HR	J	BC	DR	R	CG		HR	DR	FR	L	H	P	D		HR	L		H	D
													SO	SX	SX	SO	SX						
		a.m.	a.m.	a.m.	a.m.	a.m.	a.m.	p.m	p.m		p.m	p.m	p.m	p.m	p.m	p.m	p.m	noon	p.m			p.m.	p.m
LONDON (King's Cross) .... dep.		4 45	7 15	7 15	10 10	11 20	11 30	1 30	1 40	...	4 0	5 30	5 45	1045	1045	1045	10 45	12 0	10 45			10 45	10 5
														a.m	a.m	a.m	a.m						
Ben Rhydding	arr.	10 12	—	12E36	3H36	—	5H15	—	—		3 52	—	11A46	7 52	7 52	—	—		7 52	—		7 52	—
Ilkley	"	10 15	—	12E39	3H41	—	6H18	—	—		9 55	—	11A49	7 55	7 55	—	—	p.m.	7 55	—		7 55	—
Harrogate	"	10 44	1K40	1243	2E43	3 3	5 47	—	5 10		8 51	10 0	10E20	4 38	6 22	3 8 15	5 15		4 38	—		6 22	8 15
Ripon	"	12 5	1N50	2 39	4 43	3 25	—	7 11	—		9 13	—	11A27	3 6	55 8	36	7N54	5 43	5 3	—		6 55	8 40

									WEEKDAYS										SUNDAYS			
		HR	H	DR	EG	ME	EFR	DR		BC	HR	J	DR	D	H	SO		HR			H	H
																						D
		a.m.	a.m.	a.m.	a.m.	a.m.	a.m.	p.m.		p.m	p.m	p.m	p.m	p.m	p.m	p.m		Y	NR			
Ripon .... dep.		—	7 20	7 54	9 0	10 0	1144	12¼ 5		12 58	1 50	2 52	—	7N11	9 20	9 20		a.m.	a.m.		a.m.	a.m.
Harrogate	"	6 30	7 55	8 33	9 35	11 15	1230	12T46		1 52	2 27	4E45	5 8 8	5 9	44	10 35		—	8 36		9 52	7 33
Ilkley	"	6 14	—	—	6R12	—	1037	—		—	2 22	4H 0	—	—	7 57	—		8 32	—		10 30	8 18
Ben Rhydding	"	6 17	—	—	6H16	—	1040	—		—	2 25	4H 3	—	—	8 0	—		—	—		—	—
													a.m.	a.m.	a.m.						
LONDON (King's Cross) .... arr.		11 35	1 5	1 35	1 55	3 20	5 10	6 15		—	4 45	7 22	9 25	10 53	35 35	5 55		3 45	5 15		5 55	3 33

27. LNER timetable.

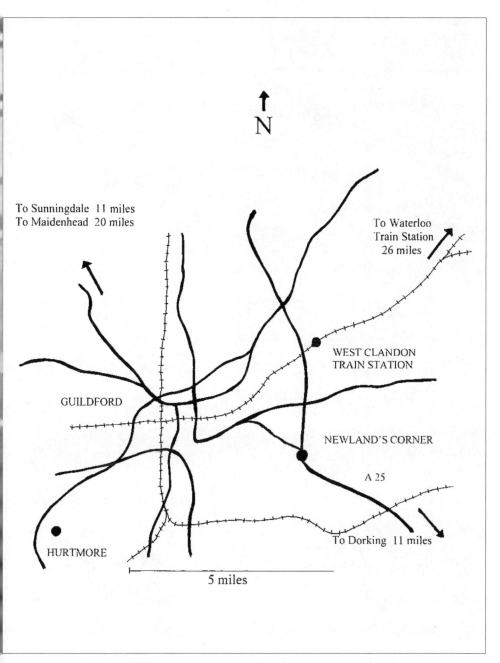

N

To Sunningdale 11 miles
To Maidenhead 20 miles

To Waterloo
Train Station
26 miles

WEST CLANDON
TRAIN STATION

GUILDFORD

NEWLAND'S CORNER

A 25

To Dorking 11 miles

HURTMORE

5 miles

28. Map of Newlands Corner.

29. The Swan Hotel, Harrogate, previously known as 'The Hydro', where Agatha stayed in December 1926.

As already mentioned, for Agatha herself, the night terrors had ceased in childhood. Nonetheless, the memory of them remained with her. Now, and only now, is it possible to comprehend the terrible agony suffered by Agatha in the long months leading up to her disappearance, and the mental scarring which her divorce from Archie left behind.

Celia and Larraby talked throughout the night; he being afraid that she might make an attempt to commit suicide by leaping out of the window – the bedroom being on the fourth floor. Although the couple were in Celia's hotel bedroom, nevertheless, Larraby's concern for her overrode his sense of propriety. His purpose was to salvage her life. As for his reputation, this was of secondary consideration.[6]

At 7 o'clock in the morning, Larraby left her. She was lying on her side and sleeping like a child. He believed that the danger had now passed, that the burden had been taken from Celia's shoulders and placed upon his. She was now safe. Then suddenly, when the pair were saying goodbye to one other on the boat that was taking them off the island, a climax occurred in Celia's life. From having the appearance of 'a tired child – obedient and very sweet and completely bemused', Larraby observed that she suddenly seemed to awake from her slumbers and saw *him* for the very first time. When Celia complained that she did not even know his name, he declined to give it, saying that it did not matter, as it would mean nothing to her. All he confided to her was that he was once a moderately famous painter of portraits. But he was not a portrait painter now. And why not? Because of something that had occurred during the war. She asked what that was, whereupon he thrust forward his stump, *'where the hand ought to have been'*.

The sound of the bell meant that Larraby had to depart, and when he did so, the impression that he was left with was one of *'horror'*, followed by *'relief'*. And yet it was more than relief . Perhaps *'deliverance'* would be a better word. The Gun Man, Celia's 'symbol for fear', had plagued her all through the years, but now she had met him in the flesh. And he was no more than a plain human being. *'Me…'*. This was Larraby's view of the situation. As for the future, he firmly believed that Celia could now go back home, and at the age of thirty-nine, begin a new life once more, leaving 'her story and her fear' with him.

Larraby now lost touch with her. Just as she did not know his name, neither did he know hers. So he called her Celia, a name which he conjured up for her because it seemed suitable. He could have found out more about her, but he felt unable to do so. He supposed that he would never see her again.[8]

Unfinished Portrait is clearly an allegorical story in which Larraby, a portrait painter, produces a portrait of Celia, not in oils or watercolours, but in words which he has constructed himself from what she has told him of her life. It is by necessity unfinished, in that Celia is a comparatively young woman whose life has still some distance to run. Similarly, when he reveals the stump where his missing hand should be, he is forcing Celia to confront her worst fear, that of The Gun Man, for it is only by so doing that she can overcome her nightmares and insecurities.

It is pertinent to ask, did the character of Larraby in *Unfinished Portrait* have any basis in reality? Was there a knight in shining armour who suddenly appeared to rescue Agatha, the damsel, from her distress? A possible answer to this mystery may lie in the visit Agatha made with Rosalind and Carlo to the Canary Island of Las Palmas in February 1927, only a few weeks after her disappearance and car crash.

Agatha writes of Las Palmas in glowing terms; describing it as being her ideal place to visit in the winter months. It was here, in the evenings with Carlo, presumably when Rosalind was tucked up in bed, that she made friends with a Dr Lucas and his sister Mrs Meek. The doctor was a specialist in the treatment of tuberculosis, having himself been crippled during his youth, possibly from this disease, or possibly from poliomyelitis, and left with a hunch-back.

Agatha described Dr Lucas as a highly successful doctor who was a 'born healer'. The doctor's family called him 'Father', and soon she and Carlo found themselves doing the same. When Agatha consulted him about a sore throat from which she was suffering, he realized that something was troubling her and asked her what it was. Could it be, perhaps, to do with her husband? She confirmed that this was indeed the case, and explained the situation to him. Dr Lucas was cheery, stimulating, and positive. Archie would come back to her if she wanted him too, provided that he was given sufficient time. The important thing was, that when he did come back, she did not reproach him. Agatha did not share the doctor's optimism, feeling that her husband Archie, was not the type to come back. At this, the doctor impressed on Agatha how important it was, that whatever happened she must face matters and go forward. After all, she was strong enough and brave enough for something good to come out of her life – even now. 'Dear Father, I owe him so much. He had enormous sympathy for all human ailments and failings,' said Agatha. When, some five or six years later the doctor died, Agatha felt that she had lost one of her best friends.[9]

Therefore, just as Larraby came to Celia's rescue in *Unfinished Portrait*, it seems distinctly possible that it was Dr Lucas who came to Agatha's rescue in similar circumstances. This, despite a small difference in the dates: whereas Agatha met Dr Lucas in February 1927, in *Unfinished Portrait* Celia describes herself as aged thirty-nine when she met Larraby. (Substituting Agatha for Celia, this corresponds to the year 1929). This discrepancy of two years has a possible explanation in that Agatha refers to Dr Lucas as one of her best friends. This implies that the two of them kept in touch after they returned to England. So, did Dr Lucas continue to try to help Agatha, and did he succeed two years later in 1929, by finally making her confront her fears, and thereby rid herself forever, of her memories of The Gunman? Was the doctor the real 'portrait painter'?

Whatever the truth of the matter may be, Agatha appears to have returned from Las Palmas in a more positive frame of mind. When she returned to England, she declared that she felt herself again. She had toughened herself up, learned to be more wary of the world, and believed that she was now better equipped to cope with all it could throw at her.[10]

A perusal of the *Medical Directory* for the year 1927 gives more details of Dr Lucas, the proverbial 'knight in shining armour' who apparently rescued Agatha, the 'damsel in distress'. His first name was Geoffrey. His address: Cook's Hill, Mundesley, Norfolk, and his telephone number was Mundesley 4. He studied at Cambridge, Durham, and St George's Hospital, London, and having worked at the Nordrach Sanatorium, Banchory near Aberdeen, Scotland, was currently the Resident Physician at the Mundesley Sanatorium. (This was without doubt the sanatorium on the east coast to which Agatha refers in her autobiography; Mundesley being situated on the coast of Norfolk, about 18 miles from its county town of Norwich).

From Agatha's account, Dr Lucas was a man of great kindness and humanity. He was also a distinguished physician, being a Fellow of the Royal Society of Medicine, with papers entitled 'Climate of Deeside' (published in *Journal of Tuberculosis*, and probably relating to the efficacy of that region's particular climate in restoring the health of the tuberculosis suffers in the sanatorium at Banchory where he worked); 'Treatment of Dry Pleurisy by Temporary Partial Artificial Pneumothorax', and 'Treatment of Pulmonary Tuberculosis by Nitrogen Compression' (both published in the *British Medical Journal*).[11]

Agatha's observation about Dr Lucas, that he was hunch-backed, having been crippled in youth, suggests that he may have suffered from tuberculosis of the spine, or Pott's Disease, which is common in the age group 1-20 years. By destroying one or more of the spinal vertebrae, typically in the thoracic region, the tubercle bacillus may cause a deformity. Could this be the reason that the doctor chose to make tuberculosis his speciality – in that he himself was a victim of it and on this account, wished to help others with the same condition?

Agatha's continuing recovery is attested to, by what she said in anticipation of a forthcoming visit to the Middle East in 1928. There came a time in life when one had to go on alone. This was something she had never previously had to contemplate, and she confesses to a certain degree of reluctance. Nevertheless, she faced a stark choice. She could either carry on in the old way, and 'cling to everything that's safe', or else she could attempt to 'develop more initiative', and plough her own furrow, so to speak.

27

Motivation, Inspiration, Perspiration

Amazingly, despite all the upheavals in her life, Agatha's writing continued unabated, with a total of eleven major novels and short story collections published in the 1920s. However, to say that she was driven by some kind of work ethic would be untrue. In fact, as Agatha says, she could never understand why people always tended to assume that there was something praiseworthy meritorious about indulging in hard work.[1] No, her motives were far more down to earth than that. Looking back, she affirmed that the good part about writing in those times was that she directly related it to earning money. For example, it was her wish that the conservatory be demolished and converted to a loggia in which they could sit. But how much would it cost? Having asked for an estimate, she then sat down at her typewriter, where she planned the layout of the story that was establishing itself in her imagination. She duly wrote it, and in consequence, she was able to afford her loggia.[2]

Also, for Agatha, writing was of secondary importance to her domestic duties. Something to be kept firmly in its place. Say, for example, she was filling in a form which asked her what her occupation was. The only answer, as far as she was concerned, was to write 'married woman'; for this was her status, and this was her occupation, and she was proud of it. The writing of books was only a sideline!

As for authorship, she points out that there is a difference between being a novice on the one hand, and becoming a more seasoned writer on the other. In the early stages, it was all too easy to become carried away in one's admiration for a favourite author. However, it does not follow that just because that style suits them, it will necessarily also suit you. In fact, the adoption of another writer's style may actually be detrimental to one's own writing. As time goes by, admiration for other writers becomes less of an influence.[4]

Here, Agatha is describing what every writer goes through in the process of discovering, to coin a phrase favoured in literary circles, 'his or her own voice'. As for what inspired her literary creations, she disclosed how plots came into her mind at unexpected times. For example, when she was walking along a street, or looking in a shop window. A 'splendid idea' would then enter her head, as to how the criminal, having committed the crime, then went on cunningly to disguise his action in such a way that nobody would be able to discover a motive for it.[4]

Agatha often wondered where her ideas came from, but whatever their source may have been, there was no denying that feeling of intense pleasure which the moment of pure creation provided. It was then that she felt 'nearest to God'. She had been able to create something that was outside of herself, and because of this she felt 'a kinship with the Almighty', as he himself may have felt on the seventh day, when he saw that what he had made was good.[5] (In fact, in The Bible, Genesis 1.31., it was on the sixth day when 'God saw every thing that he had made, and, behold, *it was* very good').

Writing, however, was no picnic for Agatha, especially when she embarked upon a new novel, and was consequently forced to endure what she described as a 'terrible' period of 3 weeks to a month, as she tried to get started on it. During this agonizing time, she would sit in her room, gnaw at a pencil, stare vacantly at the typewriter, walk aimlessly about, feeling all the time that she wanted to cry. Plays, on the other hand, she found much easier to write because she could visualize them in her mind's eye, and was not burdened with having to write long, descriptive passages, which 'clogs' an author so dreadfully in their writing, and prevents them from getting on with the story.[6]

Fortunately for her reading public, Agatha did continue to knuckle down and get on with the job in hand; continuing in each new work to bring in as background those everyday things that were important to her. As crime writer Val McDermid said, her readers did not mind being scared as long as they were scared safely, and part of that safety was encapsulated by Miss Marple's peonies and homemade scones, or M. Poirot's light-hearted witticisms about what he perceived as English eccentricity – such ingredients serving in Agatha's novels as enduring reassurances, no matter how many murdered bodies were found in the library, or on the Orient Express.

28

Homeliness, Tradition and Village Life

To know Agatha's novels is to know Agatha the person, because, as already stated, those things which were important to her, inevitably, found their way into her writings.

Comparing Hercule Poirot with Miss Jane Marple, it is clear that the lifestyle of the latter approximates, far more closely, to that which Agatha enjoyed, or would have liked to enjoy. Not for Miss Marple the fine wines and exotic repasts to which Poirot was accustomed – but rather homemade cakes and scones. In *4.50 from Paddington* Miss Marple, in order to calm her friend Mrs McGillicuddy, who has just been witness to a murder, prescribes, 'a glass of my cowslip wine', with the promise, perhaps later, of 'a cup of camomile tea'. In *At Bertram's Hotel*, it was said of Miss Marple that the idea of attending a fashion show of any kind would simply not have occurred to her. What she did enjoy were visits to department stores, and in particular to their glass, china, and household linen departments. In other words, she was a home-maker.

Christmas for Agatha was a particularly special time, as indicated in *The Adventure of the Christmas Pudding*, when government official Mr Jesmond invites Poirot to an old-fashioned, rural, English Christmas. According to Mr Jesmond, this was a custom that was dying out. Nowadays, people preferred to spend this seasonal time in a hotel. But it was his opinion nevertheless, that nothing could beat 'an English Christmas' with all the family, the children included, congregating in order to enjoy Christmas stockings on Christmas Eve, the Christmas tree, the turkey and plum pudding, the crackers, and the snowman in the garden. That was what he relished most.

Finally, Poirot accepts the invitation (his brief being to locate a ruby which has disappeared) and is welcomed by his hostess Mrs Lacey. Her family was as old-fashioned as it was possible to get, she said. In fact, her husband lived entirely in the past. She then proceeded to describe the plum pudding which contained, in addition to its normal ingredients, items deliberately mixed in with it for the consumers to find, including a 'bachelor's button' – a button in the shape of a buttercup – and a number of sixpences. However, sixpences were now no longer used on account of them not being made of pure silver any more. Mrs Lacey positively drooled when she recollected the desserts they had enjoyed in times gone by, together with luxuries such as Elvas plums, Carlsbad plums, almonds, raisins, and crystallized fruit and ginger. And finally, she apologized for sounding like 'a catalogue from Fortnum and Mason!'

When Poirot duly discovers the aforesaid bachelor's button in *his* portion of plum pudding and is told, that this means he is destined forever to be a bachelor, he entirely concurs.

As for Miss Marple, it is clear that time has brought certain changes of which she does not approve. In *A Murder is Announced*, she declares that the village of Chipping Cleghorn where the story is set, is very much like St Mary Mead, where she herself lives. Only fifteen years ago the inhabitants – families such as the Bantrys, the Hartnells, the Price Ridleys, and the Weatherbys – were all known to one another; their relatives having lived in the village for many generations. Nevertheless, there was the occasional newcomer: perhaps someone who had served in the same branch of the armed forces as one of the villagers, who would observe the correct etiquette by introducing himself formally, and perhaps bring with him letters of introduction to guarantee his bon fide. On the other hand, if a total stranger arrived, the villagers would naturally be curious, even suspicious, and they would do all they could to establish that person's credentials. In other words, he or she would be noticed. Normally, however, it was only possible to form an opinion about these 'strangers' by what they cared to divulge about themselves. Sadly, it was now the case that every village and hamlet had become inundated by people who had no ties or kinship whatsoever with those already there.

Not only that, but the physical structure of the village had changed. The large houses had been put on the market, and the cottages converted for the use of the newcomers. The result was that nobody actually knew anymore, who anybody was.

However, even in these changed times, for those coming to the village and embarking on village life, a degree of conformity had still to be observed. For example, when in *The Moving Finger*, Jerry Burton and his younger sister Joanna rent a house 'Little Furze', at Lymstock on the edge of the moors, Jerry remarks on the latter's clothes, declaring that her 'skirt of outrageous and preposterous checks', which is 'skin-tight', together with her 'sheer silk stockings and some irreproachable but brand new brogues', are quite inappropriate for the country. What would be appropriate, as far as her attire was concerned, would be a tweed skirt, preferably old, worn, and of a subdued colour; a matching cashmere jumper, and possibly a cardigan coat. And to accompany this, a suitably subdued hat, stockings, and shoes – and, preferably, old ones at that'. Then, and only then, would she blend in to the background of Lymstock High Street, and not stand out as she did at present. He also rebukes Joanna for wearing too much make-up.

Agatha subtly used the charm and tranquillity of her country village locations to best advantage, by beguiling her readers, prior to pitching them headlong into the drama which is about to unfold. In *The Moving Finger*, Joanna describes the village of Lymstock to her brother Jerry, as being charming, amusing, and 'old-world' in character. It was impossible to think of 'anything nasty' happening there, wasn't it? Again, in *The Cornish Mystery*, Hastings describes a house in Cornwall belonging to Edward Pengelley and his wife; the latter having appealed to Poirot in the belief that her husband was trying to poison her. The house, with its traditional cottage garden at the front, was set back some distance from the road. In the evenings, the scent of stocks and mignonette came floating on the air. It seemed quite preposterous to imagine any violence occurring amidst this 'Old World charm'.

One can almost hear the bees buzzing in Miss Marple's garden, and the rustle of her housemaid's dress as she brings out the tea tray; as the church clock strikes the hour and the errand boy whistles to himself as he rides by, his bicycle tyres making crunching noises on the gravel path. What better devices could Agatha have employed to heighten the feeling of anticipation in her readers, who trust, implicitly, that she will not disappoint them, and that within a few turns of the page there will be a murder most foul?

29

Gardening and Flowers

Flowers feature strongly in Agatha's books, both before and after her divorce from Archie, indicating, that despite the trauma, her capacity to derive pleasure from beautiful objects remained undiminished.

One of her earliest memories was of the wallpaper in her nursery at Ashfield where she was born and grew up, with its mauve irises which appeared to ascend the walls in a seemingly limitless fashion.[1] In childhood she enjoyed visits to Ealing, to her maternal great-aunt Margaret Miller, in whose garden there were more flowers to be seen. This pleasure she would recall in her later years, remembering the scent of roses which assailed her as she left the house via the side door. Grannie was inordinately proud of her roses, attributing all their size and beauty to 'the bedroom slops, my dear. Liquid manure – nothing like it.'[2]

When Agatha and her former husband Archie, moved into a rented flat in Sunningdale in 1924, again, it was floral designs which she chose for the décor. Her dining room curtains were emblazoned with tulips on a white background – a pattern which she had fallen in love with. In Rosalind and Swite's room which was larger, the theme was buttercups and daisies. For her own bedroom, Agatha chose a bluebell pattern. For Archie's dressing room, and the emergency spare room, the curtains were festooned with scarlet poppies and blue cornflowers.[3] It seems likely, therefore, that in Agatha's house, there were as many flowers inside as there were outside!

Agatha's love of flowers is also evidenced by the frequency with which she mentions them in her novels, and in particular those featuring her alter ego Miss Marple. For example, in *At Bertram's Hotel,* the latter describes the extremely pleasant bedroom that they had provided her with, where the wallpaper was patterned with roses, and also the en-suite bathroom where there was a similar pattern on the tiles.

Neither is Miss Marple averse to getting her hands dirty. She compares Bertram's Hotel, which she describes as the nerve centre of one of the largest and most impressive crime syndicates that had existed for many years, to a herbaceous border. Should that border become victim to a severe infestation with ground elder – a plant with spreading, underground stems – then there was no alternative but to uproot all the plants, dig it over, and start again. Likewise, in *4.50 from Paddington*, when Mrs McGillicuddy arrives at Miss Marple's house and tells her friend that she had just been witness to a murder, the conversation quickly reverts to the subject of gardens. Rising from the table, Miss Marple declares that peonies are unpredictable. They may thrive, or they may not. But if they do, then the owner of the garden will have the pleasure of them for ever, and what exquisite varieties there were to choose from nowadays! A little later, Miss Marple complains that because of her advancing years, she had been unable to give her garden the attention it deserved. However, there was nothing she could do about it – her doctor having strictly forbidden her either to stoop or to kneel, and if one could do neither, then it was hopeless.

In *Sleeping Murder*, Miss Marple comes to the rescue with the aid of insect repellent. Gwenda Reed is at her home Hillside, and her guest Miss Marple, is in the garden. Dr Kennedy arrives and enters the house. Gwenda suspects him of murder and confronts him with her suspicions. The doctor's hands fasten around Gwenda's throat. Then, suddenly, he stops in his tracks with a gasp, as a jet of soapy water strikes him in the face and eyes, and he hears Miss Marple, who is somewhat short of breath, having hurried, and only just arrived in the nick of time. How fortunate, she says dryly, that at that moment, she had just been syringing her roses in order to kill the greenfly.

Miss Marple is not the only one amongst Agatha's characters to appreciate flowers. *The Body in the Library*, for example, opens with the words, 'Mrs Bantry was dreaming. Her sweet peas had just taken a First at the flower show.' Similarly, when in *A Pocketful of Rye* Lance Fortescue asks his wife Pat, what she would plant in an English garden, she replies, hollyhocks, larkspurs and Canterbury bells. There would be no bedding plants, and no yew tress, which she absolutely detested.

Flowers also were to feature in the story *Yellow Iris,* in which Poirot is summoned, urgently, to a restaurant by a woman Pauline Weatherby, who informs him that her life is in danger. She tells Poirot that he will be able to identify her, as she will be sitting at a dinner table decorated with yellow irises. It transpires that the dinner table has been booked by Barton Russell, who has invited the same five guests whom he entertained exactly four years previously. On that occasion, Russell's wife, who was called Iris (and was the sister of Pauline Weatherby), suddenly collapsed and died on the dance floor; potassium cyanide being subsequently found in the dregs of wine in her wine glass.

Russell now tells Poirot that he believes Iris was murdered, and by someone who was then, and is now, sitting at the dinner table. Sure enough, Pauline's fears are realized when, on this occasion, an attempt which is unsuccessful, is made on *her* life. Poirot has his suspicions as to who is responsible for these dark deeds, though for once, he fails to bring the culprit to justice.

Agatha's affection for flowers remained with her all her life, as the following account reveals:

> During the years she spent at Greenway [a house situated on the banks of the River Dart which she purchased in 1938 when she was aged forty-eight], Agatha Christie and her family always turned up at the local Brixham Flower Show. For visitors [to the show] they were as much an attraction as the rows of prize-winning vegetables. She began exhibiting in the [nineteen] fifties... Each flower was especially placed so that it showed to its best advantage.[4]

Agatha entitled one of her plays *No Fields of Amaranth* – Amaranthus being a genus of flowering plant whose name derives from the Greek 'amarantos', meaning 'everlasting'. A phrase containing the word is to be found in the book by English writer Walter Landor (1775–1864), called *Imaginary Conversations* (i.e. with historical personages): 'There are no flowers of amaranth on this side of the grave'). Incidentally, Agatha's play was subsequently renamed *The Unexpected Guest*, and finally staged under the title *Verdict*.

30

Theatre and Objets d'art

As a child, Agatha created imaginary characters whose lives and adventures filled the void of loneliness in her own life. In the same vein, she acted in many childhood plays and dramas whenever the opportunity arose, and later took delight in going to the theatre. When she became a writer, she was able to give full expression to this imaginative nature of hers by creating dramas of her own: bringing inanimate objects such as ornaments and dolls to life (as in *Problem at Sea*, where a doll actually appears to speak), and by employing the artifices of costume and even of disguise.

In *Peril at End House*, there are echoes of the theatrical productions which Agatha used to stage at her childhood home Ashfield. Nick Buckley (a young lady who inherited End House on the death of her brother) tells Poirot that she loves End House, and considers it the ideal location for a play which she would dearly like to produce in this dramatic and atmospheric environment. In fact, she had already rehearsed several such plays in her imagination, which she considers might be suitable. Bearing in mind Nick's wish, Poirot announces, towards the end of the story, that yes, a play would indeed be staged at End House, but it was he who would be its producer – not Nick! In fact, the play takes the form of a séance, and with the help of Hastings, who acts the part of the medium, Poirot takes another step forward towards solving the case which he currently has in hand.

As for disguise, Agatha uses this ploy in *The Mystery of Hunters' Lodge*, where Mrs Zoë Havering, niece-in-law of the murdered Mr Harrington Pace, invents two fictitious characters with the object of putting Poirot off the scent. First, she tells Captain Hastings about a visitor who had called to see Mr Pace just before he was murdered. According to her, this person, who was of middle-age, sported a black beard, was wearing a pale-coloured overcoat, and had an American accent. However, when Mrs Middleton, a new housekeeper, arrives on the scene, Poirot's suspicions are aroused because he realizes that she and Zoë never appear together at the same time. In other words, Zoë and Mrs Middleton are one and the same person. This knowledge enables Poirot to deduce what the 'housekeeper' does when she runs upstairs on the pretext of answering a call from her mistress. In fact, she changes into a colourful jumper; dons a hat to which dark curls are attached; removes her old make-up, and applies some rouge. The transformation is now complete, and the crystal clear voice of the dazzling Zoë Havering can be heard as she descends the stairs. For Zoë, adopting a disguise presented no difficulty, for prior to her marriage her occupation had been that of an actress.

When Agatha was a child, she was fascinated and enchanted by two sets of Dresden china figurines: one possessed by her parents at Ashfield, and the other by Auntie Grannie at her home in Ealing. The title of her short story *The Affair at the Victory Ball*, refers, presumably, to a fancy dress ball held in the year 1918 to celebrate the Allied victory in the First World War. Here, Lord Cronshaw of Barclay Square possesses three pairs of china figurines in three pairs; similar to those mentioned above and based on the Italian *Commedia dell'arte* (improvised comedy which flourished in Italy from the 16th to the 18th century). These are Harlequin and Columbine, Pierrot and Pierrette, and Punchinello and Pulcinella. Of these, the romantic figure of Harlequin would undoubtedly have been of special appeal to Agatha.

Using a favourite device of hers, that of bringing inanimate objects to life, Agatha creates a scenario whereby Lord Cronshaw's party of six, go to the ball dressed in costumes which are precisely based on those of his two sets of china figurines. When Lord Cronshaw is murdered by being stabbed with a table knife through the heart, Poirot investigates, and it is by making a careful comparison of the costumes worn by those of the late noble Lord's party who attended the Victory Ball with those of the china figurines, that he is able to solve the case.

From an early age, music was another important part of Agatha's life. She learned to play the pianoforte, learned to sing, and enjoyed opera, particularly the music of Wagner. It is, therefore, not surprising that she often uses musical expressions in her writing. In *The Moving Finger* for instance, the doctor tells injured airman Jerry Burton, that he must take life gently, and at a '*tempo*' that is marked '*Legato*'.

Despite the financial insecurities of her childhood, Agatha described her household as 'a family of collectors'. Referring to her father Frederick, she spoke of the pieces of furniture which he had purchased, every one being 'a gem'. For Agatha, however, there was a drawback, in that having inherited a fine collection of ceramics and furniture, this left her with no pretext to begin collecting on her own behalf.[1] Also, she may not have shared her father's enthusiasm for what she called his 'pride and glory' – 'a stuffed bald-headed eagle' which was kept in an enormous glass case in a corner of the room.[2] On her visits to Auntie Grannie (widow of successful American businessman Nathaniel Frary Miller) at Ealing, and to her brother-in-law James Watts' family home Abney Hall, Manchester, Agatha also found herself surrounded by beautiful objets d'art which, again, she undoubtedly appreciated.

Judging by the way she introduced treasures such as these into her novels, Agatha, like her father, clearly had an eye for a fine piece of furniture, as demonstrated by her description of the dentist Mr Morley's waiting room in *One, Two, Buckle My Shoe*. The writing table was in the style of Sheraton, and the sideboard was in the style of Hepplewhite. However, she was careful to state that both these pieces were 'reproduction' and not original. There is also a description of two candlesticks of Sheffield-plate, and an epergne – ornamental centre-piece for the table. As for the chairs, they were upholstered in material which displayed a motif of birds and flowers dating from the Jacobean period.

In *The Moving Finger*, there is a certain snobbishness about Mr Pye, the dilettante resident of Prior's End, Lymstock, who looks down on the villagers there; describing them as having no sense of taste. He remarks, scornfully, that in his opinion, they are not only 'painfully bucolic', but also '*provincial*'. To mix furniture up in such a way was a positive crime. A piece by Sheraton, for example, which any collector would have been delighted to get his hands on, should in no way be placed next to such items as a Victorian occasional table, or a fumed oak revolving bookcase. Mr Pye emphasized the words *fumed oak*, in order to demonstrate his absolute disdain of people so lacking in taste as to behave like this.

Agatha's main love appears to be for china. In *A Murder is Announced*, a pair of Dresden china lamps in the shape of a shepherd and a shepherdess prove important to Miss Marple in her investigation into the death of a young man called Rudi Scherz, receptionist at the local Royal Spa Hotel. In her endeavours to solve the mystery, Miss Marple recalls a vital clue given to her by another murder victim Dora Bunner, companion to Miss Letitia Blacklock, who had hinted that the Dresden lamp in Miss Blacklock's drawing room (which was the scene of the first murder) was changed on the day the man with the gun had burst in and shot Scherz. Miss Bunner was able to affirm that whereas it was the shepherdess lamp which had been in situ on the day of the hold-up, she had noticed that the next morning, that had disappeared and been replaced by the other lamp – i.e. the shepherd lamp. This change had apparently been effected during the night. From this, Miss Marple deduces that the murderer had tampered with the 'shepherdess lamp' in order to fuse the lights of the household and thereby conceal his, or her identity.

There are further references to china in *The Moving Finger*, where Miss Emily Barton of Lymstock is described as of a deep pink colour, and 'very Dresden'. When Jerry and Joanna Burton rent Miss Barton's house from her, the latter's maid Florence, stays on to look after them and on one occasion, enters the room bearing a tea tray, the cups of which are of Crown Derby manufacture.

Nursery Rhymes, Poetry and Literature

The nursery rhymes which Agatha had learned as a child continued to fascinate her as an adult, and she made good use of them in novels such as *A Pocketful of Rye*:

Sing a song of sixpence, a pocketful of rye,
Four and twenty blackbirds baked in a pie.
When the pie was opened the birds began to sing.
Wasn't that a dainty dish to set before the king?

The king was in his counting house,
counting out his money,
The queen was in the parlour
eating bread and honey,
The maid was in the garden
hanging out the clothes,
When there came a little dickey bird
and nipped off her nose.

(N.B. This is Agatha's version of the rhyme. There are others.) Sure enough, in the story, when the first victim Rex Fortescue is murdered, seeds of the cereal rye, are found in the pocket of his jacket. The second victim dies after eating (poisoned) honey; the third is found dead with a clothes peg clipped to her nose. Agatha's famous female sleuth, who in her own words, had been 'brought up on Mother Goose' realizes that the whole case revolves around the nursery rhyme. Rex, the Latin word for 'King', is an allusion to the king in his counting house. Mrs Adele

Fortescue is a representation of the queen in the parlour eating her bread and honey. And Gladys, the Fortescues' parlour maid, equates to the maid in the poem who, instead of having her nose nipped off, has a clothes peg placed on it by the murderer. But what is the relevance of the blackbirds, as mentioned in the poem? Miss Marple suggests to Inspector Neele, that this would be a subject worthy of further investigation.

The final part of the mystery is solved when the housekeeper Mary Duff, tells the inspector that someone had previously left four dead blackbirds on the desk in Mr Fortescue's study. Neele also learns that some were left on the library table, and also put in a pie. Finally, it is Rex Fortescue's son Lancelot, who provides the answer, when he reveals that the late Rex Fortescue and a man called MacKenzie, were involved in the workings of the 'Blackbird Gold Mine' in East Africa.

What made Agatha decide to call the police inspector in her novel 'Neele' – this being the surname of her former husband Archie's mistress Nancy, whom he had married shortly after his divorce from Agatha? Was it because, despite the passage of time, the name had remained embedded in her subconscious for twenty-five years (whereas Agatha's divorce occurred in 1928, *A Pocketful of Rye* was not published until 1953), or was this Agatha shrugging her shoulders and saying to the world, this is a name that I simply treat as any other nowadays?

Likewise, in *How Does Your Garden Grow*, Poirot arrives at the house Rosebank, belonging to the murdered Amelia Barrowby, to discover a flower bed which is partly edged with shells. This puts him in mind of the nursery rhyme:

> Mistress Mary, quite contrary,
> How does your garden grow?
> With cockle-shells and silver bells,
> And pretty maids all in a row.

(Again, this is Agatha's version of the rhyme.) Sure enough, an attractive little maid, with lustrous blue eyes and ruby cheeks answers the front door, and it subsequently transpires that the shells in the flower bed were from oysters, used by the murderer as a vehicle to administer strychnine to his victim.

The novel *One, Two Buckle My Shoe*, is again based on a children's nursery rhyme, and features an ornate shoe buckle which is crucial in determining the identity of a murdered woman.

Agatha's novels, and also her biography, are liberally sprinkled with poetical quotations and imagery; for poetry was a subject close to her heart and one in which she was well schooled. In *The Moving Finger,* Megan Hunter, who had previously rejected the advances of injured airman Jerry Burton, saying that she was not in love with him, has a change of heart and writes him a letter. She has been re-reading one of Shakespeare's sonnets, one that she was familiar with when a schoolgirl (actually Sonnet No.75), which begins with the words:

So are you to my thoughts as food to life
Or as sweet-season'd showers are to the
ground.

Which makes her realize, because of the sentiments expressed therein, that she *is in fact* in love with him.

The title of Agatha's novel *Absent in the Spring* also derives from a Shakespearean sonnet (No.98), 'From you have I been absent in the Spring…'.

Nurse Amy Letheran, in the novel *Murder in Mesopotamia*, refers to a poem by John Keats, again one which she had been familiar with in childhood. The poem keeps coursing through her mind, and she is desperately trying, but without success, to remember its exact words. Could it be: '*Oh say what ails thee, knight at arms, alone – and* (what was it?) *– palely loitering…?*' (In fact, the poem actually reads: '*Oh, what can ail thee, Knight at arms / Alone and palely loitering…*').

The 'knight at arms' referred to by Amy is Doctor Richard Carey, the expedition's archaeologist, who she described as having 'a grim, tense, bronzed face' and she felt sorry for him because he reminded her of the soldiers whom she remembered from the days of the 1914-18 War.

Agatha, in her autobiography, also quotes Keats, in what is a poignant reference to her traumatic divorce from Archie:

What shall I do to drive away
Remembrance from mine eyes?

Agatha's love for the written word is revealed by the frequency with which literary quotations appear in her novels. For example, in *At Bertram's Hotel*, the honourable Elvira Blake, the beautiful young daughter of Lady Bess Sedgwick, murders Michael Gorman, Bertram's Hotel's doorman. Referring to this fact, Miss Marple comments on the beauty of 'The children of Lucifer', who, as everybody knew, thrive 'like the green bay tree'. (These words derive from the Prayer Book of 1662: 'I myself have seen the ungodly in great power: and flowering like a green bay tree').

In *Murder on the Orient Express*, the conductor of the Simplon Orient Express informs Poirot that there is one passenger, an Englishman named M. Harris, who has not yet boarded the train. Poirot believes that this is an excellent portent, the name being mentioned in a novel by Charles Dickens, with which he is familiar. (In fact, it is a reference to a female character who appears in *Martin Chuzzlewit*).

In the same story, M. Bouc, a Belgian who is director of the Compagnie Internationale des Wagons Lits, contemplates the breakfast table. If he only had the talent of French novelist Honoré de Balzac, he would definitely make a record of this scene. When the American Samuel Edward Ratchett is subsequently murdered, Poirot considers the possibility that not one, but two persons may be responsible for the crime. He drew an analogy to the 'great' William Shakespeare's play *Macbeth*, which, amongst its characters, features the First and Second Murderer.

The Bard of Stratford-upon-Avon is quoted once again in *The Body in Library*, when Miss Marple and Sir Henry Clithering, a former Commissioner of Scotland Yard, hatch a plot to catch the murderer of Girl Guide Pamela Reeves. She says she is doing so, in order to be absolutely quite *sure* of the murderer's identity, or, in the words of Macbeth, again in Shakespeare's play of the same name, to 'make assurance doubly sure'.

Agatha's Own Views

From the pronouncements of the characters in her novels, perhaps it is possible to deduce a little of what Agatha's own opinion was on the merit, or otherwise, of the great writers. If so, some, it appears, she loved unreservedly; others made her irritable and impatient. Certainly, she had little time for what she regarded as the minutiae of the art.

In *The Moving Finger*, for example, Megan Hunter describes English grammar as 'rot', and composition as 'silly'. Just as the poet Percy Bysshe Shelley was over sentimental about skylarks; so Wordsworth, in her opinion, was excessively romantic about 'some silly daffodils'. As for Shakespeare, his writings were often so convoluted that it was all one could do to understand what he was driving at. Megan did admit, however, that she did like '*some* Shakespeare'. In the same story, Joanna Burton indicates that she too has reservations about Shakespeare, describing him as invariably 'terribly dreary'. The scenes of his plays were excessively long, and not improved by the fact that everyone was always drunk. She did not find this amusing.

When in *A Murder is Announced*, Edmund Swettenham is paying court to Phillipa Haymes, he advises her that the poet Alfred Lord Tennyson, is shortly to make a comeback in a big way. He tells her that the *Idylls of the King* – a series of related poems about the legendary King Arthur and his Knights of the Round Table – is currently being serialized on the wireless. This was infinitely preferable to the 'interminable' Anthony Trollope, whose prose he had always considered to be a 'most unbearable affectation'. Some Trollope was permissible, but one could have too much! He then compares Phillipa to Tennyson's character *Maud* in the Monodrama – i.e. a dramatic piece for one performer – of the same name. In his opinion, Phillipa is 'Faultily faultless, icily regular', and 'splendidly null.'

32

A Fascination with Trains

When Agatha was young, steam trains were in their heyday, carrying both passengers and goods to virtually any location of meaningful size in the land. Towards the end of her long life, however, the steam train had been relegated to a few scenic branch lines, run by charitable trusts to serve as tourist attractions, and manned by volunteers who were, largely, unpaid.

As a child, Agatha would have been aware that the Great Western Railway (GWR) line and Torre Station were within easy walking distance of her family's home Ashfield, with Torquay Station a mile or so away and nearer the sea. It was not until the mid-1920s (when she was in her thirties) that Agatha acquired a motor car for the first time. Up until then, for overland travel, beyond the confines of her home town, she would have been dependent on the train. So what possibilities did the GWR have to offer?

Agatha's local railway (constructed in 1848) runs from Torquay across country for 6 miles to Newton Abbot; then skirts the northern edge of the estuary of the Teign River to Teignmouth, from where it continues around the coast and western side of the estuary of the Exe River to Devonshire's county capital city Exeter (the line from London having reached Exeter in 1844). This route ranks among the most picturesque in Britain. Alternatively, from Newton Abbot it was possible to travel south-westwards around the southern edge of Dartmoor to the port of Plymouth. Agatha acknowledged that there was still a certain romance attached to ships, even in the age of the aeroplane, but what could beat a train, and especially that particular type of train which preceded those smelly, diesel-powered ones of which she so disapproved? How she admired the 'great puffing monster' of former times, which could transport one to wild and spectacular countryside. 'Trains are wonderful; I still adore them,' she said.[1]

Trains feature in many of Agatha's stories: one of the most celebrated being entitled 4.50 *from Paddington*. In the novel, Mrs Elspeth McGillicuddy sets off a few days before Christmas on this very train from London's Paddington Station (real life) to visit her friend Miss Marple. As another train, also on the down-line, pulls alongside, she sees a man in one of its compartments standing with his back to the window. His hands were gripping the throat of a woman whom he was steadily, and dispassionately strangling. Finally, the train stops at Milchester Station, where a taxi takes Miss McGillicuddy on to Miss Marple's home village of St Mary Mead. 'Oh Jane!' she says, 'I've just seen a *murder*!'

In the absence of a corpse to corroborate Mrs McGillicuddy's story, and faced with a somewhat sceptical police force, Miss Marple decides to investigate the matter for herself. First, in order to establish 'the *terrain* of the crime', she and Mrs McGillicuddy retrace the journey that the latter took when she witnessed the murder. With the help of her nephew's son David West, who worked for British Railways, Miss Marple realizes that the train which overtook Elspeth's on that fateful day was either the 4.33 or the 5.00 from London. She also obtains some useful maps of the area from the vicar's son Leonard, who has a passion for cartography. Finally, because Mrs McGillicuddy is adamant that the carriage which passed her did not have a corridor, Miss Marple is able to narrow the possibilities down to one, i.e. the 4.33 Swansea Express. Accordingly, she sets off for London once again, and this time catches this very same 4.33 train. As it nears Brackhampton, Miss Marple notices that it is obliged to slow right down, owing to the sharp curvature of the line.

Such painstaking research leads Miss Marple to think that the body of the murdered woman must have been thrown out of the train as it slowed down on its approach to Brackhampton, and to prove it, she enlists the support of the highly intelligent young Lucy Eyelesbarrow, who, despite having a First Class degree from Oxford, prefers to work as a locum housekeeper. She, therefore, suggests to Lucy that she apply for such a post at Rutherford Hall – the grounds of which are adjacent to the railway line. 'I want you to find a body,' says Miss Marple. And this is precisely what Lucy does.

Railway timetables also held a fascination for Agatha: the times of arrival and departure of trains often being crucial to the plot. (In those days, the trains, allegedly, ran to time!) For example, her novel *ABC Murders* derives its title from the real life *ABC Alphabetical Railway Guide*. A feature of the story is, that beside the body of each of his victims, the murderer leaves the Railway Guide open at the page relevant to the place where the murder has taken place.

33

The Occult

The *Oxford English Dictionary* defines the word 'occult' as 'involving the supernatural; mystical, magical'. In her autobiography, Agatha refers to being addicted, at one time, to writing 'psychic stories', and the occult features in many of her books. (Her mother Clara is known to have attended séances, but not Agatha, as far as is known).[1] Nevertheless, despite her interest in the subject, she prefers, as will be seen, to keep her feet firmly on the ground.

As is often the case with Agatha, her novel *Unfinished Portrait* is the most revealing source of information as far as her own interest in the occult is concerned. The period referred to is one where 'Celia' (i.e. Agatha) is married to 'Dermot' (Archie) and has a little girl 'Judy' (Rosalind).

As Celia is pushing Judy to the park, presumably in her pushchair, she has a story running through her head about an imaginary girl called Hazel, which she thinks might lend itself to being made into a book. When she moots this to Dermot, he thinks it 'an excellent idea'. She tells her husband that Hazel is a medium, who happens to be unaware that she possesses mediumistic powers. Having grown up to know how simple it is to deceive the impressionable, and become established as 'a kind of witch's familiar [i.e. acquaintance]', Hazel becomes involved with a bogus fortune teller, and also attends séances at which she cheats. Celia realizes, however, that if she is to make a success of writing the book, she must first learn, in some detail, about 'spiritualism, séances, mediumistic powers, and fraudulent practices', to which end, she reads every single book on the subject that she can find. Only then does she, painstakingly, rewrite the whole of the first part of the book – a task which she finds she does not enjoy. Finally, the task becomes impossible, and the whole project is abandoned. Instead, Celia will write a story about a family of fisher-folk who live on the Cornish coast – an idea which she was already toying with in her mind.

The inference here is that Agatha, having considered the occult as a suitable subject for a novel, found that she derived no enjoyment from the writing of it, perhaps on account of her natural scepticism about the subject. Later, however, the occult was to feature strongly in many of Agatha's novels and short stories.

In *Sleeping Murder*, Giles Reed and his wife Gwenda come to England from New Zealand and buy a house called 'Hillside' at Dillmouth, on the edge of that 'still charming seaside resort…'. Gwenda however, has an inkling that she has been here before. She walks down to the lawn, but cannot understand why there are no steps where she thought they ought to be. Sure enough, some old steps, which have been covered up, are shortly discovered by the gardener Foster.

Anticipating the birth of her child, Gwenda decides that she would like some new wallpaper, perhaps a motif of poppies alternating with corn-flowers would brighten up her infant-to-be's bedroom. Yes, this would be delightful. (Here, she is echoing Agatha's own love of flowers and floral patterns). Then, in a corner cupboard in her bedroom, she discovers, to her surprise, some of the property's original wallpaper displaying poppies and cornflowers, which was exactly what she had in mind. Gwenda also decides that it would be most convenient if a doorway could be created to lead from the drawing-room into the dining-room. Again, when Mr Simms the builder, comes to effect the work he finds that there has been a door there previously, which has been plastered over. These revelations cause Gwenda to feel uneasy. She had no desire whatsoever to be a clairvoyant, and had never shown the slightest interest in anything that might be described as 'psychic'. She simply was not that kind of person. Or was she?

Most disturbing of all, is the time when Gwenda attends a performance of playwright John Webster's Jacobean tragedy *The Duchess of Malfi* in London, in the company of author Raymond West and his wife Joan, and Raymond's aunt Miss Marple. On hearing the words '*Cover her face. Mine eyes dazzle, she died young…*', Gwenda springs up from her seat and runs out of the theatre in panic. This is because, yet again, she was reminded of a former occasion, when, standing on the landing of the house Hillside, she looked down through the banisters and saw a woman lying in the hallway having been strangled.

As far as the steps, the doorway and the wallpaper are concerned, far from seeing this as an occult phenomenon, Miss Marple tells Gwenda that in her view, the explanation is quite simple. Gwenda *had* seen all these phenomena before, and how? Because it was more than likely that when her mother died, her father brought her to England, *to live in this very house* Hillside.

This in fact turns out to be the case. It also transpires that the strangled woman whom Gwenda had seen through the banisters was her mother.

In *The Sittaford Mystery*, Captain Joseph Trevelyan decides to let Sittaford House to a Mrs Willett and her daughter Violet, while he himself moves to a small, rented house on the outskirts of Exhampton. At a séance, subsequently held by Mrs Willett at Sittaford House, a spirit indicates (correctly) that Captain Trevelyan is dead, and that he has been murdered. Later still, Emily Trefusis, who is engaged to Captain Trevelyan's nephew James Pearson, declares how much he abhors 'supernatural things'. However, on this occasion, he was prepared to admit that there might be 'something in it'. To which newspaper reporter Charles Enderby answers sceptically, that if it was possible for Captain Trevelyan to contact those attending the séance, and inform them that he was dead, then why, equally, could he not say who had murdered him? What was the problem in this?

In *Dead Man's Mirror*, Vanda, the wife of Sir Gervase Chevenix-Gore, tells Poirot that her husband is the victim of fraud. The famous Belgian sleuth investigates, and is informed by Mr Satterthwaite, a guest in the house, that Vanda had always been interested in the occult, that she adorned herself with amulets and scarabs (presumably brooches in the shape of scarab beetles which were sacred to the ancient Egyptians), and led everyone to believe that she was 'the reincarnation of an Egyptian Queen…'. Sure enough, when Sir Gervase is found dead in his study, Vanda responds predictably, declaring that to her, the world of the spirits was quite as valid as the world which she inhabited. Fate had a hand in everything; it was impossible to escape from one's Karma (destiny). The episode of the mirror, which she said, was entirely in keeping with this philosophy. In this, Vanda was referring to the mirror that hung on the wall behind the desk of her late husband's study. Poirot duly asks her for an explanation, which she now gives.

The fact that the mirror was splintered was symbolic. Was Poirot familiar with Tennyson's poem which she had read in her childhood, but without realizing its significance and which she now quoted:

The mirror cracked from side to side.
'The curse is come upon me! cried the Lady of Shallott.'

Vanda believed that this explained the death of her husband Gervase. The curse, which is the bane of many of the ancient families of the land, had come upon him, and from the moment that the mirror cracked, 'he knew that he was doomed!' Poirot then remonstrates with her, saying that it was not a curse, but a bullet that had cracked the mirror. His words, however, make no impression, and Vanda carries on regardless, describing her late husband as 'one of the Great Ones born again'. Such was his status, that he now believed human beings to be foolish, not only because they believed that life was a real entity, but also because they pretended to themselves that it actually mattered; whereas, in fact, life was only a 'Great Illusion'.

Vanda then discloses to Poirot that she is a reincarnation of Hatshepsut, the Egyptian queen of the eighteenth dynasty who reigned in about 1500 BC. This leads Chief Constable Major Riddle to affirm that Vanda is even madder than he ever realized! Did she really believe in what he could only describe as 'nonsense'? Poirot, however, has an explanation. It was important at this time for Vanda to conjure up for herself 'a world of illusion', because by so doing, this would enable her to ameliorate the 'stark reality' of her husband's demise. Here, once again, Agatha, through her characters, offers a logical explanation for seemingly illogical occurrences and thought processes.

The location for *The Hound of Death* is the fictitious village of Folbridge in Cornwall, where the narrator's sister Kitty, looked after some Belgian refugees during the First World War. One of them is Sister Marie Angelique, who, at the end of hostilities, chose to remain in the area. According to Doctor Rose, Sister Marie suffers from hallucinations, and has therefore been placed under the skilled supervision of the district nurse, with whom she resides in a small cottage on the outskirts of the village.

Sister Marie describes how, when in the First World War the Germans advanced on her convent in Belgium which was obstructing their path, she unleashed the 'hound of death' by calling down lightning onto it. Furthermore, following the lightning strike which all but destroyed the building, a black powder mark in the precise shape of a huge hound was left imprinted on one of the walls which was still standing. Apparently, none of the nuns were hurt, and the local peasants, thereafter, regarded the event as a miracle.

Sister Marie confides in Doctor Rose, who discovers that her beliefs revolve around a 'crystal ball', the 'house of crystal' and the 'people of the crystal' – the crystal being a holy emblem. She tells him that she herself was a Priestess of the Fifth Sign in the House of the Crystal (implying that she had held a position of power and influence at some former time in history). She then corrects herself and says she was a Priestess of the Sixth Sign. Sister Marie then agrees to be hypnotized by Dr Rose. As a result, the latter deduces that the Sixth Sign without doubt represented the 'Power of Destruction', and that it was by invoking this power that Sister Marie had been able to destroy the convent. Doctor Rose, in his notebook, then indicates that he himself may be falling under the influence of Sister Marie's occult beliefs: '*Am I mad? Or shall I be the Superman, with the Power of Death in my hands?*'

When Mr Rose, Doctor Rose's nephew, dies after being struck by lightning, again, a mark in the shape of a hound is found imprinted on his body – as was the case with the convent following its destruction. Finally, when the doctor's cottage on the cliff is swept away in a landslide and both the doctor and Sister Marie are killed, the narrator is left wondering if these three deaths were caused by Dr Rose attempting to use the Force of Destruction for his own ends, but negligently failing to exercise proper care.

Finally, Agatha brings her readers back to earth by pouring cold water on all of these bizarre notions, when the unnamed narrator of the story declares that it is all 'nonsense', and that there was a perfectly logical explanation for everything. The doctor's belief in Sister Marie Angelique's hallucinations was merely evidence that *his own* mind was also 'slightly unbalanced'.

And yet, this is not quite the end of the story, for, in a tantalizing twist to the tale, the narrator goes on to say that often, he dreams of a continent, now submerged under the sea, which was once inhabited by men who 'attained to a degree of civilization far ahead of ours…'. This is a clear allusion to Atlantis, a continent or island mentioned in Greek mythology and said to have sunk following an earthquake.

34

Englishness

Agatha, as has been shown, loved so much of what, in her time, was regarded as being quintessentially English – village life, afternoon tea, roses, the countryside, steam trains, etiquette, good manners, a suspicion of foreigners, and so forth.

Murder in Mesopotamia begins with hospital nurse Amy Leatheran, writing a letter home from the Tigris Palace Hotel in Baghdad to Sister Curshaw of St Christopher's Hospital, London. She had appreciated seeing something of the world, but for her, England is definitely the place to be. In *A Pocket Full of Rye*, Pat Fortescue encounters Miss Marple relaxing in the library of Yewtree Lodge. She finds it pleasant enough, with the fire burning and the lamps lit, as Miss Marple sits knitting garments for infants. In fact, with its cosiness and homeliness, it was just as she thought England should be.

Referring to the maid Ellen, in *Peril at End House*, Poirot describes her as immensely 'quiet' and 'respectable' in the traditional English way. The story features Captain Seton, who is attempting a round-the-world flight in his aeroplane the *Albatross*. Events such as these made Hastings feel delighted that he was 'an Englishman after all'.

In *A Murder is Announced*, Detective Inspector Craddock describes Phillipa Haymes as, 'too wooden for Rosalind (a character in Shakespeare's *As You Like It*), her fairness and her impassivity' being typically English, but English of the present times, and not of the sixteenth century when the bard of Stratford wrote his play. As Poirot, in *Peril at End House,* debates whether Charles Vyse, a lawyer, was capable of murdering his cousin Nick Buckley, with whom he has fallen in love, rather than permit her to marry another man, Hastings remarks, 'It sounds very melodramatic'.

To which the famous Belgian sleuth agreed. Yes, it does not sound English, 'but even the English have emotions'. Similarly, in *Murder on the Orient Express*, Poirot enquires of Mary Debenham, a young English lady who is travelling home from Baghdad where she has been working as a children's governess, as to whether she is at all distressed to hear that a misdemeanour had been committed on this train? She tells him no, this is definitely not the case. She is not at all distressed. Whereupon Poirot tells her that she is 'very Anglo-Saxon', in her disapproval of emotion.

In *The Body in Library*, Miss Marple gives her views on what she considers to be good etiquette. A girl of good breeding is always careful to wear clothes that are appropriate to the occasion. No matter how hot the weather, it is definitely not the done thing for her to arrive at a point-to-point horse race meeting dressed in a flamboyant silk frock.

In the story, Miss Marple realizes that Dinah Lee is married to Basil Blake, even though she pretends not to be. She advises Dinah, in no uncertain terms, that now she is living in the village, she must discontinue the use of her maiden name. This, because people living in such old-fashioned rural locations were prejudiced against those who lived together out of wedlock.

In *Murder in Mesopotamia*, Nurse Amy Letheran notices that one of the members of an expedition to that region, Mr Coleman, has a small bunch of scarlet ranunculus (plants of the buttercup family) in his hand. She is fascinated, because she has seen these 'pretty little flowers' growing wild on the banks of the Tell [Arabic word for 'hillock']. When Coleman tells Amy that he intends to put these flowers on the grave of the murdered Mrs Leidner, wife of the expedition's leader, she regards this as a very fine gesture. She also observed him blushing as he told her his plans, as all Englishmen do when they have performed any sentimental action.

In *The Adventure of the Christmas Pudding,* Colonel Lacey of Kings Lacey is annoyed to hear that Poirot will be present at his family's Christmas festivities, and he remonstrates with his wife. Why on earth does she want what he describes as a 'damned foreigner' clogging up their Christmas? He could not stand foreigners, but if Poirot had to come, then why could he not arrive at a more convenient time? In *A Murder is Announced*, Miss Blacklock takes the opposite view, when she chastises Detective Inspector Craddock for casting aspersions on her cook Mitzi, who is a refugee from Europe. The police, she said, were guilty of having an 'anti-foreigner complex'. Even if Mitzi was a liar, she was certainly not 'a cold-blooded murderer'. In *The Moving Finger*, Miss Emily Barton complains about her stocks and shares which she had purchased on the recommendation of the bank manager, and which she had always supposed to be such a safe investment. Why did they currently produce absolutely no yield? Ah yes, it must be because they were *foreign* stocks and shares!

In 4.50 *from Paddington*, Emma, daughter of Luther Crackenthorpe of Rutherford Hall, declares that, in the absence of evidence to the contrary, she always makes a point of assuming all foreigners to be French. After all, the majority of foreigners in this country *were* French, were they not? In the *The Mysterious Affair at Styles*, John Cavendish grumbles about Dr Bauerstein, an expert on poisons. He is sick and tired of having the fellow loitering about all the time, and in particular because of the fact that he, Bauerstein, is a Polish Jew. To which his wife Mary counters, that to have *some* Jewish blood was by no means a disadvantage, as 'it leavens the stolid stupidity of the ordinary Englishman'.

And yet, having travelled widely and lived abroad, Agatha, with her keen sense of humour, was able to appreciate the English as others see them, and poke gentle fun at such English qualities as reticence, distrust of foreigners, and sang-froid (coolness and composure). In *Triangle at Rhodes*, Miss Pamela Lyall is described as unusual for an English woman, in that she has the wherewithal to engage strangers in conversation immediately, rather than wait until several days or weeks have passed before making the first timid approach.

English reserve, however, could be taken too far. In *Murder on the Orient Express*, the American/Italian Antonio Foscarelli describes Englishman Edward Henry Masterman (valet of the murdered Samuel Ratchett) with whom he shares his cabin, as a sour faced 'John Bull'. He lacks sympathy, scowls, is antisocial and refuses to hold a conversation; when he does, he speaks only in monosyllables. Instead, he prefers to nestle in his chair in the corner of the room and read. In fact, in Foscarelli's opinion, he is typical of the English race as a whole.

35

The Middle East, Max, a New Life

When, in the autumn of 1928, Agatha is invited out to dinner with friends in London, a chance meeting with a young naval officer Commander Howe and his wife, changes her life forever. Agatha, who had always been vaguely drawn to archaeology, even though she confessed to being quite ignorant on the subject,[1] is already aware of the work of English archaeologist Leonard Woolley at Ur in Iraq. Now, having extolled the virtues of Baghdad, that country's capital city from where he had recently returned, the commander suggests that she might like to travel there by train, in fact by The Orient Express.

Soon, this idea [of Howe's] becomes a reality, and having travelled to Damascus, capital of Syria, where she spends three days, Agatha finally arrives at Ur, where she is welcomed by Woolley, and by his wife Katharine (who has recently read and enjoyed Agatha's *The Murder of Roger Ackroyd*) and 'given the VIP treatment'. Katharine was to become one of Agatha's closest friends in the forthcoming years.[2] Here, she meets Maurice Vickers, an Anglo-Indian, who also becomes a friend. It was Vickers who taught her to give thought to the concept of time, something which had never occurred to her before. She found this to be highly beneficial, in that having a sense of the infinite enabled her to place personal problems, and the consequent sadness and tribulation which they caused, in a proper perspective.[3] Agatha is equally impressed by an Iraqi policeman who proceeds to recite the whole of the poet Percy Bysshe Shelley's 'Ode to a Skylark' to her in English.[4]

Katharine Woolley arranges for Agatha to visit the Iraqi cities of Nejef (the Muslim holy city of the dead), and Kerbala, which has a splendid mosque with a gold and turquoise dome.[5] For this, she is to be escorted by Max Mallowan, who for the last five years has been Woolley's assistant. This is followed by an expedition to view a crusader's castle at Kalaat Simon (Iraq).[6] At Mersin on the Turkish coast, which they also visit, Max and Agatha have a picnic and find themselves surrounded by a landscape awash with yellow marigolds, some of which he picks, makes into a chain, and hangs around her neck.[7] At this, Agatha, who loved flowers, would have been mightily impressed. It is while they were swimming in the clear blue waters of a desert lake at Ukhaidir (Iraq), that Max decides that Agatha would make a most suitable wife for him.[8]

On hearing that her daughter Rosalind is ill with pneumonia, Agatha decides that she must travel home as quickly as possible on The Orient Express. Max offers to travel with her. When Max proposes marriage, Agatha's instinct is to refuse him, for the reason that she was his senior by many years.[9] (In fact Max, born in 1904, had been a contemporary of Agatha's nephew Jack Watts at Oxford).[10] Also, Max was a Roman Catholic. Agatha confessed that re-marrying was the last thing on her mind. '*I must be safe*', she said; safe from anyone ever being able to hurt her again.[11] However, she does admit that she and Max share a great many common interests, and that to her, his work as an archaeologist is far more fascinating than any of her former husband Archie's financial transactions in the City of London.[12] Another positive factor is that Rosalind clearly likes Max, and approves of him. Finally, on 11 September 1930, the couple are married in the chapel of St Columba's Church in Edinburgh. They spend their honeymoon in Venice, Yugoslavia and Greece.

A year previously, on 20 September 1929, Agatha's brother Monty, who was in Marseilles at the time, died unexpectedly of a cerebral haemorrhage whilst at a café on the sea front. He was interred in that city's military cemetery.[13]

The play *Alibi*, performed in 1928, was the first to be produced from one of Agatha's books – *The Murder of Roger Ackroyd*. *Murder at the Vicarage*, published in 1930, was the first novel to feature Miss Marple, described by Agatha as, the kind of elderly lady who she imagined would have resembled some of my grandmother's 'Ealing cronies…'.[14] Whereas Poirot comes across as being sophisticated, fastidious, and dapper, Miss Marple contents herself with the simple pleasures of life – having a nice cup of tea, gardening, attending flower shows. Perhaps the altogether more relaxed environs in which Miss Marple operated, and the fact that she was female, made a welcome change for Agatha when it came to portraying her character.

Agatha took a keen interest in the work of her husband Max, describing the years from 1930 to 1938, when he and she were excavating in Iraq and later in Syria, as especially rewarding in that they were 'so free of outside shadows'.[15] It became the couple's habit to leave England in December or January, travel to the Middle East, and return the following March, after a season's digging.

Max's next assignment was at Nineveh (Iraq), where Agatha joined him for a dig on the Quyunjik Mound; with the River Tigris just one mile away. When Max (now assistant to Reginald Campbell Thompson) discovered the remains of the potter's shop with splendid crockery, vases, and other 'polychrome pottery all shining in the sun', which had laid untouched for about 6,000 years, Agatha felt she was 'bursting with happiness'.[16] After a period at Arpachiyah (Iraq) in 1932, Max moved to Syria: first to Chagar Bazar, and in 1937 to Tell Brak.

Meanwhile, in December 1934, the couple purchased an additional property 'Winterbrook House' at Wallingford in Oxfordshire. As for Agatha's daughter Rosalind, after leaving her girls' public school, Benenden, Kent, she spent time on the Continent and learnt to speak fluent French. On one occasion she joined Agatha and Max in Syria on a dig.

The couple finally returned to England, to Number 48 Sheffield Terrace, London; another house which Agatha owned. In 1939, Agatha and Max added yet another house 'Greenway', a Georgian mansion standing in extensive grounds, overlooking South Devon's River Dart, and dating from about 1780, to their portfolio of properties.

When the Second World War broke out, Max joined the Home Guard at Brixton, Devon, and Agatha volunteered to work once again in the dispensary at the hospital in Torquay. Later, she joined Max in London and their house Greenway, was let as a nursery for children evacuated from the St Pancras district of London. Greenway was subsequently requisitioned by the Admiralty and taken over by officers of the United States Navy. In 1940, Rosalind married Hubert Prichard, a major in the regular army. From 1940 to 1945, Max served in the Royal Air Force Volunteer Reserve as Liaison Officer with Allied forces and as Civilian Affairs Officer in North Africa.[17]

When 48 Sheffield Terrace was bombed, Agatha and Max moved to a flat in Hampstead. He was now working at the Air Ministry; she commenced work at University College Hospital. On 21 September 1943,

Agatha's grandson Mathew Prichard was born. Agatha described the boy as a most rewarding person to be in company with, and it was his 'incurably optimistic' demeanour which she found to be particularly attractive.[18] It was to Mathew that she bequeathed the play *The Mousetrap* (the stage version of *Three Blind Mice*, written to celebrate HM Queen Mary's 80th birthday in 1947). There were many other beneficiaries of Agatha's books and stories, including family and friends, and also organizations, such as the Westminster Abbey Appeal Fund and her local church at Churston Ferrers, to which she donated a stained glass window.

In August 1944, Agatha's daughter Rosalind received a telegram to say that her husband Hubert Prichard had been killed in action in France. At the end of the war in 1945, Greenway was derequisitioned by the Admiralty.

In 1947, Max, who had now been appointed Professor of Western Asiatic Archaeology at London University, returned, after an absence of ten years, with Agatha to the Middle East. Here, as Director of Iraq's British School of Archaeology, he would organize a dig at Nimrud, once the military capital of Assyria. In this project, which would take twelve years, his wife was as enthusiastic as he. Agatha proclaimed that she was unashamedly attached to the artistic and hand-crafted objects which were unearthed as the result of her husband's archaeological digs. And most fascinating of all were those objects crafted by the labour of the human hand. This included a small casket – 'pyxis' – made of ivory and carved with images of musicians and their instruments, a 'winged boy', and the bust of a woman's head which was both 'ugly', yet at the same time 'full of energy and personality'.[19]

Referring to the excavations at Nimrud, which she admitted had been defaced by their bull-dozers, Agatha declared, confidently, that before long, its scars would heal, and that the flowers that had previously grown there in early spring, would do so once again.[20] It was here that she began writing her autobiography, in addition to spending time on photography and on mending and cleaning ivories.[21]

Agatha was in her element. Referring to the people of the Iraqi city of Mosul, she commented on how good it was to have friends such as these: affectionate, unsophisticated, full of the joys of life, and with a well-developed sense of humour. Whenever she happened to travel through a village where one of their workmen had his home, he would immediately rush out and offer hospitality, demanding that she and Max join him in a drink of sour milk. How devoted she was to this region of the world. 'I love it still and always shall.'[22]

Meanwhile, in October 1948, Agatha's daughter Rosalind remarried, to barrister Anthony Hicks.

And so, at last, Agatha appears to have found that joy and contentment for which she had so long yearned; a yearning which she alludes to over and over again in her writing. For example, in her very first published book, *The Mysterious Affair at Styles*, Poirot declares the happiness of a loving couple to be the most important attribute in all the world. To which his colleague Hastings entirely concurs. In *Triangle at Rhodes*, (published in 1936), Marjorie Gold describes to Poirot, her relationship with her husband Douglas. The couple were so blissfully happy together. And bearing in mind what was going on all around them, when so many marriages were unhappy, breaking down, and often ending in divorce; well this did indeed make one feel 'grateful for one's own happiness'.

36

Middle Eastern Mysteries

Having spent a decade or more of winters in the Middle East, it is hardly surprising that Agatha wrote many novels based on this region, and from her writings it is clear that its people and their customs became very dear to her heart. It was at the suggestion of Stephen Glanville (Professor of Egyptian Archaeology and Philology at University College, London, from 1935–1946), that Agatha wrote *Death Comes as the End* (published in 1945), a detective story set in Ancient Egypt.

In *Murder in Mesopotamia* (1936), Hercule Poirot, in an effort to discover who has murdered Louise, wife of archaeologist Dr Eric Leidner, assembles all the suspects together, as is his custom. He then begins his address to them by quoting a phrase in Arabic, 'Bismillahi ar rahman ar rahim,' which he translates into English: 'In the name of Allah, the Merciful, the Compassionate.'[1] (Each chapter of the Koran begins with these words). Agatha gives a detailed description of the expedition house with central courtyard containing bedrooms, dining room, photographic room and dark room, including laboratory, antika room (presumably one where ancient exhumed artefacts were stored), and drawing office. Outside were dormitories for the native servants; a guard-house for the soldiers – there, presumably, to protect them and the site. There were stables for 'water horses' – those used to transport that most vital of desert commodities, water.[2] There are also descriptions of workmen, attired in threadbare garments with bandages around their heads, such as a person might wear if he or she had a toothache. Agatha observed that many workmen suffered from severely discharging eyes, and that a couple appeared to have almost lost their sight.[3]

There are references to pots; an exquisite golden dagger, its handle set with precious stones, and an equally exquisite golden drinking-vessel, embossed with figures of the heads of rams. This cup, which was unique and dated from the Early Akkadian Period (Akkad – a northern Semitic people who conquered the Sumerians in 2350 BC and ruled Mesopotamia), was described as one of the most beautiful ever found anywhere in the world.[4] All these artefacts were excavated from the grave of a prince.

The pots were cleaned by pouring a solution of hydrochloric acid over them. There were references to removing dust from a skeleton that had just been unearthed, and to brushing and cleaning all the bones and all the objects with a knife, and keeping them in position ready to be photographed (a process in which Agatha, no doubt, enthusiastically participated).[5] Also to 'inscribed bricks' and 'cylinder' seals (tablets or barrel-shaped objects of stone or baked clay respectively).[6]

The novel *Murder on the Orient Express* (1934) is centred on the train which took Agatha for her first visit to the Middle East, and which she would take many times subsequently. Similarly, *Death on the Nile* (1937) is set aboard the steamer *SS Karnak* as it embarks on a Nile cruise. *Come, Tell me how you Live* (1946), an autobiographical account of Agatha's life with Max at their archaeological camp headquarters in Syria, was given by Agatha as a present to Max on his return from the Second World War.

37

Faith, Good and Evil

Agatha was brought up in a Christian household, although, for her mother Clara, choosing a religion was a far from simple process. This was because, in Agatha's words, Clara had 'a naturally mystic turn of mind', which made finding the particular type of religion which suited her, a problem. She tried theosophy, the Unitarian Church, Roman Catholicism, and even Buddhism; dragging her reluctant husband along with her on the journey.[1] However, Agatha's father Frederick, whom she described as an uncomplicated, conventional Christian, was relieved when Clara returned to the Church of England in time for their daughter Agatha to be christened in the Parish Church.

Clara and Frederick Miller originally intended that their third child be baptized 'Mary Clarissa', 'Agatha' being added only 'as an afterthought'; the name having been recommended to Clara by one of her friends as they were en route to the church![2] As for Agatha's religious views, she would be influenced in this mainly by Nursie, whom she describes as a 'Bible Christian'. Nursie being a person who did not go to church but preferred to read her Bible at home.[3]

One of the teachers at Agatha's first school in Torquay made a great impression on her by describing what Christianity should mean to the individual. In order to be a Christian, it was necessary to experience the same type of life that Christ himself lived; to enjoy what he enjoyed, to feel the same happiness that he felt at the marriage of Cana (when he turned the water into wine for the guests); to know the contentment and joy which being at one with God and with his commandments can bring. One must also experience, as Christ did, what it means to be on one's own in the garden of Gethsemane (situated near Jerusalem where

Christ prayed), in the knowledge that all your friends have abandoned you, including those whom you loved and trusted, and that this even applies to *God Himself*. In those circumstances, it was essential to keep on believing that this was '*not the end*'. To love was to suffer, and those who did not love would never know the meaning of what it is to be a Christian.

Agatha told how those simple words made more of an impression on her than those of any sermon that she had ever listened to. In fact, they remained with her, to be recalled many years later as a source of hope and comfort, at a period when 'despair had me in its grip'.[4]

Her Christian faith and devoutness did not prevent Agatha from writing in humorous vein in her novels about the ecclesiastical life of the village. For instance, when Griselda Clement, the vicar's wife, announces in *The Murder at the Vicarage* that she is to entertain some guests at the vicarage (Miss Marple included), she anticipates 'Tea and scandal at four-thirty'. Sure enough, when the time comes, Griselda has some important news to impart to the assembled company regarding Mrs Lestrange, a new arrival at St Mary Mead. She could confirm, that this newcomer to the village was the wife of a missionary. And not only that, but the Reverend Lestrange had suffered a terrible fate. She was able to divulge what she knew as fact, that the poor man had been eaten, actually eaten, following which event his wife had been made to become the principal wife of the chief.

As a writer of detective stories, Agatha invented frightening, and sometimes dangerous, but above all exciting, situations to the delight of millions of her readers. She creates such an atmosphere in *The Murder on the Links*, where the rambunctious Marthe Daubreuil (real name Bella Duveen) is discussing a murder with Captain Hastings. 'Well, if that doesn't beat the band!', she says excitedly, and then demands that the captain show her 'all the horrors…'. Crimes were a great passion of hers, and how fortunate that she had met Hastings in this way. She would not rest until the captain had shown her 'all the sights', which even included the body of the murdered person. However, for Agatha, fiction was in no way to be confused with reality. In fact, her attitude to real-life crime and the criminal may come as a surprise to those who think that the 'Queen of Crime' is a soft touch. In her early years of writing detective stories, Agatha was not disposed to contemplate crimes in any serious way. Instead, her interest was predominantly with the chase – the pursuit by the detective of his quarry. However, beneath each story lay a concept of morality, 'the hunting down of Evil and the triumph of Good'. This was the period of the 1914-18 War, when those who performed acts of evil were not regarded as heroes. This was a time before people had begun to immerse themselves in psychology.

However, having written a number of crime books, Agatha's thoughts turned inevitably to the subject of criminology. In her view, people who kill are evil, and bring nothing to the community except hatred, whilst, on the other hand, taking from it all that they can She thought it possible, that such people are born with some intrinsic disability which makes them behave in the way they do, but even if they are to be pitied, she did not think that they should be spared. It was of paramount importance that the innocent should be protected, in order that they could live in an atmosphere of peace and goodwill with their neighbours. It disturbed Agatha that nobody seemed to care about the innocent victim and share in their agony. Instead, people's pity was for the killer, especially if he or she was a young person.[6]

What was to be done about those who were 'tainted with the germs of ruthlessness and hatred', who considered other peoples' lives of no value? Was there a cure for their wickedness? In particular, what was to be done with a murderer? Agatha saw life imprisonment as punishment that was inappropriate: it being even more barbaric than the 'cup of hemlock' which was offered in Ancient Greece. In her opinion, transportation (i.e. to the colonies) had been the best answer to the problem, though of course, this was no longer feasible. Agatha considered that sentencing of such 'creatures' to a period of community service was a good idea. Or alternatively, he or she could be offered the choice between taking poison, or volunteering to subject themselves to medical research, where having a human being on whom to test out new drugs was of the greatest importance. Should criminals survive being used as human guinea pigs, then they would have redeemed themselves and could now go forth free men, with the mark of Cain removed from their foreheads. Perhaps Wickedness may find its physical cure – they can sew up our hearts, deep-freeze us – some day they may rearrange our genes, alter our cells.[7]

Although Agatha's solutions seem somewhat drastic, many of the concerns that she raises are equally relevant today, where the fight against crime seems to many to be a losing battle. Agatha was ahead of her time in suggesting that there may be a genetic basis for criminality –

certainly the recidivistic nature of some criminals and their failure to show the slightest remorse for their dark deeds, suggests that this might be so. Doubtless, science will provide the answers in due course, and with them, perhaps a medically based 'cure'.

In Agatha's novels, one way for a criminal to redeem himself is by performing a brave deed, as in *A Murder is Announced,* when Detective Inspector Craddock challenges Mrs Phillipa Haymes over her account of her husband's death. She had told him that her husband Ronald, described as a former captain in the 'South Loamshires', had been killed whilst fighting in Italy (i.e. during the Second World War). However, he knew for a fact that this was not true, and that instead, Haymes had deserted from his regiment. Haymes is exonerated however, when, in saving the life of a child by snatching it from beneath the wheels of a moving lorry, he himself is run over and killed in the process.

Detective Inspector Craddock mentioned this piece of gallantry, on the part of Haymes, to his superior Chief Constable Rydesdale, saying that he was pleased that Haymes had exonerated himself, not only for his wife Phillipa's sake, but also for the sake of their son, who now need no longer be ashamed of his father.

Those guilty of the most serious crimes, however, must not be seen to escape justice, even on the rare occasions when they manage to escape conviction and sentence by the courts. In *The Mystery of Hunters' Lodge*, the couple Zöe and Roger Havering conspire to murder their wealthy uncle Harrington Pace, in order to inherit his vast fortune. Poirot fears there will not be enough evidence to secure a conviction, and this proves to be the case. Nevertheless, as Hastings points out, having read an article on the subject in the newspaper, they both met their 'nemesis' when the aeroplane on which they were travelling to Paris crashed and they were found to be among those killed.

38

Latter Years

Agatha described her play *Witness for the Prosecution* (1948) as being not only the one that she liked best, but also the one, that of all her plays, she felt most satisfied with.[1] Despite her increasing success, however, the shyness that had been the bane of her life, remained with her. Having attended the opening night, she crept away, just as soon as the curtain had come down. It was to no avail, because members of the public caught sight of her. They surrounded her car, uttered words of encouragement and requested that she sign their autograph books. The effect of this warm welcome on Agatha was dramatic, and just for once, she found that her 'self-consciousness and nervousness' had evaporated.[2] In 1956 HM Queen Elizabeth II appointed her CBE.

Nancy Christie (*née* Neele) died in 1958. When, on 2 December 1959, Agatha's sister-in-law and great friend, Nan Kon (*née* Watts, who was two years her senior) died, Agatha was devastated. Although their relationship had initially been one of mutual hostility, Agatha subsequently revealed that Nan was one of her friends who she now missed more than any-body. There was, practically, no one else but Nan with whom she could reminisce about Abney Hall, the Watt's home in Cheshire, and Ashfield, Agatha's own home; of their pet dogs; the 'pranks' that they got up to; the young men who courted them, and the plays which they had performed together.[3]

In *A Murder is Announced*, Miss Letitia Blacklock voices the same feel-ings about her former companion, the murdered Miss Dora Bunner, whom she described as her only connection with the past, the only per-son who '*remembered*'. Now that Dora had departed, she felt absolutely and completely alone. Miss Marple understood and concurred with these sentiments only too well. Whereas she had several relatives of the younger generation and some dear friends, there was nobody still alive who remembered her as a child. No one, in fact, who belonged to what she nostalgically referred to as the old times.

Again, in *At Bertram's Hotel*, Miss Marple reflects that for her own part, she had been obliged to spend a large portion of her life recollecting past enjoyments. And if someone could be found who could recall them with her with equal joy and enthusiasm, then that could be called happiness indeed.

On 20 December 1962, Agatha's first husband Archie died aged 73. That year, she was invited to attend a party to celebrate the tenth anniversary of the opening of her play *The Mousetrap*. When she arrived twenty minutes early and was refused admission, she 'retreated'. Why? All she needed to have done was to have revealed her identity – apparently she was not even recognized! – and inform the manager that she had permission to enter the theatre. What prevented her from doing this? Again, it was because of what she herself described as her 'miserable, horrible inevitable shyness'.[4]

Finally, having gained entrance, she said modestly (in reference to what was to become the longest running play of all time), 'People like it, but who can say why?' When asked, 'How many years would you give *The Mousetrap* yet?' she replied with a charming smile, 'I wouldn't like to prophesy. I've always said, it's coming off [stage] next year... but it never does!'[5]

In 1965, Agatha donated the sum of £310,000 to the Harrison Homes for Elderly Ladies of Limited Means (of which there were eighteen in the London suburbs of Kensington and Hammersmith). This was followed by further gifts totalling £50,000.[6]

When in 1968, Max was knighted, Agatha became Lady Mallowan. In 1971, her eightieth year, Agatha was appointed DBE. In her lifetime, Agatha's published works included eighty-four detective novels, 136 short stories, six romantic novels and two autobiographical works. She also wrote eighteen plays.[7] By the year 2005, an estimated 2.3 billion of her books had been sold worldwide. And yet she always displayed a curious ambivalence vis-à-vis her herself and her writing. She was making a pretence of being something that she was not, and it seems scarcely credible that, even after all the years and all the success, she still did not feel as if she was an author. 'I still have that overlag of feeling that I am *pretending* to be an author,' she said.[8]

Epilogue

Agatha Christie was a person to whom home, family, her nanny, and pets were all important: friends also, although sadly, in her young life, she tended to be somewhat isolated from the outside world, as already described. These deep feelings of attachment made her particularly vulnerable to loss of any kind.

The importance to her of Ashfield, the family home in Torquay, is demonstrated by the fact that she hung on to it long after her mother's death when she could ill afford to do so; the cost of its maintenance and upkeep being enormous. Nonetheless, she had no regrets on this score. Whereas some might have considered her foolish to maintain it, yet it provided her with something of worth, 'a treasure of remembrance',[1] something that she held dear. Subsequently, wherever she lived, Ashfield remained, throughout her life, her idea of home.

Anything that threatened her safe, some might say cocooned, existence was therefore a source of anxiety; something which could even precipitate one of those night terrors from which she suffered as a child. The repeated bouts of ill health which afflicted both her parents, epitomized such a threat. When she was aged eleven, Agatha's father Frederick – 'the rock upon which the home is set'[2] – died, after which she meandered around the house in a condition of mental turmoil. This was indeed a calamity. This was something which she had never anticipated could happen.[3] When her mother Clara suffered a series of severe heart attacks, Agatha describes getting up at night, creeping along the corridor, kneeling down by her mother's bedroom door with her head to the hinge where a reassuring snore would comfort her. However, if no snoring was to be heard, she would remain at the door in a crouched position, feeling not only dejected, but intensely afraid.[4] When her beloved 'Nursie' retired, she described this as 'the first real sorrow of my life…'.[5] But there was a more sinister burden which she was also obliged to bear: that of The Gunman who always seemed to be lingering about, haunting her and threatening to replace one or other of those whom she held most dear.

Repeatedly, both in her autobiography and her books, Agatha describes how friends are so vitally important; particularly those of long standing. She was equally attached to her pet dogs, and to her budgerigar Goldie, and was distraught when the latter disappeared one day for a short period, describing it as 'the supreme catastrophe'.[6] She cried tears of relief when the creature reappeared alive. Cruelty to animals was something that she could not bear, in any shape or form.

When Agatha went on her world tour with Archie and Major Belcher, she described how travel often elicited feelings of homesickness and aloneness, and a yearning to meet up again with some person whom she held dear, in particular her mother Clara.[7]

From an early age, Agatha made it clear that her main ambition was to achieve a happy marriage and be part of a happy family – such as she had enjoyed as a child. She was a quintessentially homely person who took up writing not for its own sake, but firstly in response to a challenge from her sister Madge, and subsequently, purely to earn money.

When she met Archie, she truly believed that her dream of marital happiness had come true. When he demanded a divorce, this to her, was an event of such cataclysmic proportions that it temporarily unbalanced her mind; sending her into shock, and precipitating what today is called a psychogenic fugue. At the time, the art of psychiatry being less advanced than it is now, nobody realized or could accurately diagnose from what she was suffering. Nowadays, one would hope that she would have been treated more expertly, and perhaps with greater understanding and compassion.

What are today's parents to deduce from Agatha's experiences? How can a balance be drawn between, on the one hand, their natural instinct to protect the child, and on the other, the need to avoid being overprotective? In a rare criticism of her own upbringing, Agatha (through 'Celia' in *Unfinished Portrait*) declared that the balance had been wrong. Her home had been 'too happy', and as a consequence, she had grown up to be 'a fool'. In other words, her childhood days at Ashfield had not prepared her for the real world outside. For example, her parents appear never to have argued. Celia, on the other hand, heroine of her novel, *Unfinished Portrait*, regarded family squabbling, perhaps, as something of value, because it teaches children what life is really about.

Miraculously, Agatha survived the mind-blowing trauma of divorce, and continued to employ her wonderful gift, enabling millions of people throughout the world to look forward to the next Poirot or Marple novel. Finally, having shaken off memories of the sinister Gunman, she put the past behind her, and was able to flourish with her second husband Max in an entirely more amenable environment than had been the case with Archie.

In the final phase of her autobiography, Agatha quotes the words of the poem by Thomas Hood:

I remember, I remember, the house where I was born....

It was to Ashfield that she always returned in her mind.

O ma chère maison, mon nid, mon gîte
Le passé l'habite... O! ma chère maison...

How much that home meant to her. In her dreams, she seldom dreamed about Greenway or Winterbrook. Instead, it was almost invariably about Ashfield, the 'old familiar setting' where her life had 'first functioned'.[8]

When Agatha heard that her former family home was to be pulled down and a new estate developed on the site, she decided to summon up her courage and drive up Barton Road where, to her horror, she found that all the great trees, including the beech, the Wellingtonia, the pines, the elms, and the ilex, together with the ash trees in the wood, had disappeared. All that remained was a stunted monkey puzzle tree which was barely surviving in someone's backyard. There was no garden, let alone any grass to be seen. Everything had been asphalted over, and another link with the past had gone forever.

Those who were privileged enough to be introduced to Agatha at the twentieth anniversary celebrations of her play *The Mousetrap*, where she spoke so unaffectedly and smiled so charmingly, would have been entirely unaware of what she had suffered in earlier years, when the 'slings and arrows of outrageous fortune' impinged so brutally upon her highly sensitive nature. Nonetheless, as author Janet Morgan points out, her kindly nature prevailed:

> Agatha was generous to children – and to adults, for she loved giving: benefactions to her small cluster of charities; unexpected presents, a guitar, a camera, opera glasses, a fishing rod, a thirty-six-piece dinner service for a wedding present, baby clothes… Copies of [Harold] Pinter's plays and Jane Austen's novels, pieces of Lalique glass… A squash court for Mathew, treasures to old friends, spring bulbs, powder puffs, glasses, real sponges…[10]

Agatha's autobiography concludes on a happy note, evoking memories of that wonderful sense of humour and engaging smile of hers:

> Two summits of ambition fulfilled: dining with the Queen [Elizabeth II] of England; and being the proud owner of a bottle-nosed Morris – a car of my own!

Nursie, had she lived, would have been absolutely delighted, said Agatha who, with regard to the former event, finds herself unable to resist quoting the words of the nursery rhyme 'Pussy cat, pussy cat where have you been?' (which continues, 'I've been to London to see the Queen!').[11]

Agatha died on 12 January 1976 at Winterbrook, aged eighty-five, having been married to Max for forty-five years. She is buried at nearby Cholsey village. On 13 May, a memorial service was held for her at London's St Martin-in-the-Fields. Her autobiography was published, posthumously, the following year.

Notes

Introduction

★ signifies a television documentary.

1. ★Flight, Collette (Producer), *Agatha Christie: A Life in Pictures.*

Chapter 1: The Miller Family

1. Christie, Agatha. *An Autobiography*, p.13.
2. Morgan, Janet. *Agatha Christie – A Biography*, p.2.
3. Matthew, HCG and Brian Harrison (eds.). *Oxford Dictionary of National Biography*, Vol.2, p.528.
4. Christie, op.cit., p.19.
5. Ibid, p.14.
6. Matthew, op.cit., p.528.
7. Christie, op.cit., p.116.

Chapter 2: Early Life

1. Christie, Agatha. *An Autobiography*, pp.56,47.
2. Ibid, p.66.
3. Ibid, pp.45, 46.
4. Ibid, p.82.
5. Ibid, p.95.
6. Ibid, p.24.
7. Ibid, p.29.
8. Ibid, p.112.
9. Ibid, p.137.
10. Ibid, p.111.

Chapter 3: A Love of Storytelling

1.   Christie, Agatha. *An Autobiography*, p.49.
2.   Ibid, p.85.
3.   Ibid, p.109.
4.   Morgan, Janet. *Agatha Christie – A Biography*, p.76.
5.   Christie, op.cit., p.128.
6.   Ibid, p.50.

Chapter 4: A Creative Imagination

1.   Christie, Agatha. *An Autobiography*, pp.20-22.
2.   Ibid, pp.32,33.
3.   Ibid, p.105.
4.   Ibid, p.58.
5.   Ibid, p.60.

Chapter 5: The Allure of Danger

1.   Christie, Agatha. *An Autobiography*, p.54.
2.   Ibid, p.77.
3.   Ibid, p.78.
4.   Ibid, p.35.
5.   Ibid, p.121.
6.   Ibid, p.182.
7.   Ibid, p.193.
8.   ★Warwick, Ben (writer and producer). 2005. *The Agatha Christie Code*. 3DD Productions.

Chapter 6: Terrifying Dreams

1.   Christie, Agatha. *An Autobiography*, p.36.
2.   http://www.drhull.com/EncyMaster/N/night_terrors.html 17.01.2006 encyclopae-diaindex.
3.   Christie, op. cit., p.36.
4.   Ibid, p.36.
5.   Hoover, John H. *John Bowlby on Human Attachment*, http://www.cyc-net.org/cyc.online/cycol-0304-bowlby.html 18.01.2006.
6.   Hoover, op.cit.
7.   Christie, op.cit., p.153.
8.   Ibid, p.25.
9.   Ibid, p.15.

Chapter 7: Who was The Gunman?

1.   Christie, Agatha. *An Autobiography*, p.104.

2. Ibid, p.105.
3. Ibid, p.116.
4. Hall, Calvin S, *The Meaning of Dreams*, p.30.
5. Christie, op.cit., p.35.
6. Perelberg, Rosine Josef. *Dreaming and Thinking*, p.106.
7. Ibid, p.76.
8. Ibid, p.125.
9. Ibid, p.84.

Chapter 8: Writing, Music and Drama

1. Christie, Agatha. *An Autobiography*, pp.99,101.
2. Ibid, pp.123-24.
3. Ibid, p.203.
4. Ibid, pp.156-59.
5. Ibid, pp.165,188-89.
6. Christie, Agatha. *An Autobiography*, p.195.
7. Ibid, pp.130-31.
8. Ibid, pp.172,175,177.
9. Ibid, pp.200-01.
10. Ibid, p.217.

Chapter 9: Archie

1. Christie, Agatha. *An Autobiography*, p.208.
2. Ibid, pp.134-35.
3. Ibid, p.64.
4. Ibid, p.220.
5. Ibid, p.227.
6. ★Flight, Collette (producer). *Agatha Christie: A Life in Pictures*.
7. Christie, op.cit., p.227.

Chapter 10: Brother Monty and the First World War

1. Christie, Agatha. *An Autobiography*, pp.332-33.
2. Ibid, p.236.

Chapter 11: The Dispensary and the First Book

1. Christie, Agatha. *An Autobiography*, pp.257-8.
2. Ibid, p.260.
3. Ibid, pp.261-2.
4. Ibid, p.263.
5. Ibid, p.261.
6. Ibid, p.284.

7.   Ibid, pp.138–39.
8.   Ibid, p.261.

Chapter 13: Married Life with Archie

1.   Christie, Agatha. *An Autobiography*, p.271.
2.   Ibid, p.273.
3.   Ibid, p.282.
4.   Ibid, p.322.
5.   Ibid, p.291.
6.   Ibid, p.287.
7.   Ibid, p.292.

Chapter 14: More Ingredients for Stories

1.   Christie, Agatha. *An Autobiography*, p.148.
2.   Ibid, pp.145-6.
3.   Ibid, p.137.

Chapter 15: Rosalind

1.   Christie, Agatha. *An Autobiography*, p.45.
2.   Ibid, p.318.

Chapter 16: Literary Success but Problems Loom

1.   Christie, Agatha. *An Autobiography*, p.307.
2.   Ibid, p.314.
3.   Ibid, p.321.
4.   Ibid, pp.319-20.
5.   Christie, Agatha. *An Autobiography*, p.326.
6.   Ibid, p.330.
7.   Ibid, p.343,345.
8.   Ibid, pp.346,347.
9.   Ibid, pp.349,351.
10. Ibid, p.131.
11. Ibid, p.353.
12. Ibid, pp.353, 356.
13. Ibid, p.357.
14. Ibid, p.359.
15. Ibid, p.361.
16. Cade, Jared. *Agatha Christie and the Eleven Missing Days*, p.239.
17. Christie, op.cit., pp.369,363.

Chapter 18: Agatha Disappears

1. *The Times*, 8 December 1926.
2. Statement of Deputy Chief Constable William Kenward, Surrey Constabulary, Guildford, Surrey, to AL Dixon Esq., C.B., O.B.E., Home Office, Whitehall, London SW1, 9 February 1927. (Courtesy of the National Archives, Kew, Surrey, UK.)
3. *Harrogate Advertiser*, 18 December 1926.
4. Statement of Deputy Chief Constable William Kenward, op.cit.
5. Ibid.
6. Ibid.
7. Ibid.
8. *Daily Mail*, 10 December 1926.
9. Statement of Deputy Chief Constable William Kenward, op.cit.
10. *Harrogate Advertiser*, 18 December 1926.
11. *Daily Mail*, 15 December 1926.

Chapter 19: The Mystery Deepens

1. *Daily Mail*, 10 December 1926.
2. *Daily Mail*, 15 December 1926.
3. Statement of Deputy Chief Constable William Kenward, Surrey Constabulary, Guildford, Surrey, to AL Dixon Esq., C.B., O.B.E., Home Office, Whitehall, London SW1, 9 February 1927.
4. *Daily Mail*, 10 December 1926.

Chapter 20: Agatha is Found

1. *Harrogate Herald*, 15 December 1926.
2. Ibid.
3. *Daily Mail*, 10 December 1926
4. Robyns, Gwen. *The Mystery of Agatha Christie*, p.64
5. *Daily Mail*, 15 December 1926.

Chapter 21: Agatha's Own Story

1. *Daily Mail*, 16 February 1928.
2. Christie, Agatha. *An Autobiography*, pp. 359-60.
3. *Harrogate Herald*, 15 December 1926.
4. Statement of Deputy Chief Constable William Kenward, Surrey Constabulary, Guildford, Surrey, to AL Dixon Esq., C.B., O.B.E., Home Office, Whitehall, London SW1, 9 February 1927.

Chapter 22: From Styles to Harrogate: A Reconstruction of the Journey

1. Statement of Deputy Chief Constable William Kenward, Surrey Constabulary,

Guildford, Surrey, to AL Dixon Esq., C.B., O.B.E., Home Office, Whitehall, London SW1, 9 February 1927.
2. Ibid.
3. Christie, Agatha. *An Autobiography*, p.365.

Chapter 23: Agatha Transformed

1. *Harrogate Advertiser*, 18 December, 1926.
2. *Daily Mail*, 15 December 1926.
3. *Harrogate Herald*, 15 December 1926.
4. Robyns, Gwen. *The Mystery of Agatha Christie*, p.75.
5. *Daily Mail*, 15 December 1926.
6. *Daily Mail*, 16 February 1928.
7. *Harrogate Herald*, 15 December 1926.
8. *Harrogate Advertiser*, 18 December, 1926.
9. *The Times*, 17 December 1926
10. *The Times*, 17 December 1926
11. Cade, Jared. *Agatha Christie and the Eleven Missing Days*, p.141.
12. ★Flight, Collette (producer). *Agatha Christie: A Life in Pictures*.

Chapter 24: The Mystery Solved?

1. Kumar, Parveen and Michael Clark (eds). *Clinical Medicine: A Textbook for Medical Students and Doctors*, p.937.
2. Semple, David, Roger Smyth, Jonathan Burns, Rajan Darjee and Andrew McIntosh. *Oxford Handbook of Psychiatry*, p.156.
3. ★Warwick, Ben (writer and producer). 2005, *The Agatha Christie Code*, 3DD Productions.
4. Gelder, Michael, Dennis Gath and Richard Mayou. *Oxford Textbook of Psychiatry*, p.206.
5. Griffin, Georgia. *Dissociative Fugue and the Conscious/Unconscious Chasm*, http://serendip.bynmawr.bdu/bb/neuro/neuro05/web2/ggriffin.html, 06.12.2005.
6. Gregory, Richard L. *The Oxford Companion to the Mind*, p.197.
7. Information supplied by the Old Swan Hotel, Harrogate – formerly the Harrogate Hydropathic Hotel.
8. ★Flight, Collette (producer). *Agatha Christie: A Life in Pictures*.
9. Morgan, Janet. *Agatha Christie – A Biography*, p.159.

Chapter 25: Divorce

1. Christie, Agatha. *An Autobiography*, pp.423,424.
2. Morgan, Janet. *Agatha Christie – A Biography*, p.192.

Chapter 26: Recovery

1. *Daily Mail*, 16 February 1928.
2. Westmacott, Mary. *Unfinished Portrait*, pp.15,16.

3. Ibid, pp.15–6.
4. Ibid, pp.247–48.
5. Ibid, p.250.
6. Ibid, p.18.
7. Ibid, p.19.
8. Ibid, pp.251,252.
9. Ibid, p.370.
10. Ibid, p.366.
11. The *Medical Directory (Provinces)*, 1927.
12. Ibid, p.372.

Chapter 27: Motivation, Inspiration, Perspiration

1. Christie, Agatha. *An Autobiography*, p.133.
2. Ibid, p.426.
3. Ibid, p.445.
4. Ibid, p.421.
5. Ibid, p.518.
6. Ibid, pp.490,491.

Chapter 29: Gardening and Flowers

1. Christie, Agatha. *An Autobiography*, p.26.
2. Ibid, p.40.
3. Ibid, p.338.
4. Robyns, Gwen. *The Mystery of Agatha Christie*, p.221.

Chapter 30: Theatre and Objets d'Art

1. Christie, Agatha. *An Autobiography*, p.69.
2. Ibid, p.53.

Chapter 32: A Fascination with Trains

1. Christie, Agatha. *An Autobiography*, p.228.

Chapter 33: The Occult

1. ★Warwick, Ben (writer and producer), 2005, *The Agatha Christie Code*, 3DD Productions.

Chapter 35: The Middle East, Max, a New Life

1. Christie, Agatha. *An Autobiography*, p.372.

2. Ibid, pp.387-388.
3. Ibid, p.390.
4. Ibid, p.408.
5. Ibid, p.404.
6. Ibid, p.414.
7. Ibid, p.417.
8. Ibid, p.409.
9. Ibid, p.429.
10. Ibid, p.432.
11. Ibid, p.429.
12. Ibid, p.430.
13. Ibid, p.395.
14. Ibid, p.449.
15. Ibid, p.483.
16. Ibid, p.479.
17. Matthew, HCG and Brian Harrison (eds.). *Oxford Dictionary of National Biography*, Vol 36, p.347.
18. Christie, op. cit., p.521.
19. Ibid, p.542.
20. Ibid, p.546.
21. Ibid, p.544.
22. Ibid, pp.547-48.

Chapter 36: Middle Eastern Mysteries

1. Christie, Agatha. *An Autobiography*, p.162.
2. Ibid, p.28.
3. Ibid, p.38.
4. Ibid, p.40.
5. Ibid, p.131.
6. Ibid, p.136.

Chapter 37: Faith, Good and Evil

1. Christie, Agatha. *An Autobiography*, p.92.
2. Ibid, p.223.
3. Ibid, p.23.
4. Ibid, pp.153-54.
5. Ibid, p.452.
6. Ibid, pp.452-53.
7. Ibid, p.455.

Chapter 38: Latter Years

1. Christie, Agatha. *An Autobiography*, pp.532-33.
2. Ibid, pp.534-35.

3. Ibid, pp. 119-120.
4. Ibid, p. 535.
5. ★ Warwick, Ben (writer and producer). *The Agatha Christie Code*. 3DD Productions.
6. Robyns, Gwen. *The Mystery of Agatha Christie*, pp. 213-215.
7. Wynne, Nancy Blue. *An Agatha Christie Chronology*.
8. Christie, op. cit., p. 536.

Chapter 39: Epilogue

1. Christie, Agatha. *An Autobiography*, p. 118.
2. Ibid, p. 116.
3. Ibid, p. 113.
4. Ibid, p. 120.
5. Ibid, p. 47.
6. Ibid, p. 25.
7. Ibid, p. 317.
8. Ibid, p. 549.
9. Ibid, p. 550.
10. Morgan, Janet. *Agatha Christie – A Biography*, p. 330.
11. Christie, op. cit., p. 551.

Bibliography

Cade, Jared. 2000. *Agatha Christie and the Eleven Missing Days*. London and Chester Springs: Peter Owen.

Cantu, Robert C. 2001. *Posttraumatic Retrograde and Anterograde Amnesia: Pathophysiology and Implications in Grading and Safe Return to Play. Journal of Athletic Training*; 36(3):244-248. http://www.pubmedcentral.nih.gov/articlerender.fcgi?artid=155413

Christie, Agatha. 1993. *An Autobiography*. London: Harpercollins Publishers.

Glaister, Professor John. 1921. *A Textbook of Medical Jurisprudence and Toxicology*. Edinburgh: E & F Livingstone.

Gelder, Michael, Dennis Gath and Richard Mayou. 1989. *Oxford Textbook of Psychiatry*. Oxford, New York, Melbourne: Oxford University Press.

Gregory, Richard L. 1987. *The Oxford Companion to the Mind*. Oxford, New York: Oxford University Press.

Griffin, Georgia. 2005. *Dissociative Fugue and the Conscious/unconscious Chasm*. http:// serendip.brynmawr.edu/bb/neuro/neuro05/web2/ggriffin.html.

Hoover, John H. 18.01.2006. *John Bowlby on Human Attachment*. http://www.cyc-net.org/ cyc.online/cycol-0304-bowlby.html

Kumar, Parveen, and Michael Clark (eds). 1994. *Clinical Medicine: A Textbook for Medical Students and Doctors*. London: Baillière Tindall.

Daily Mail. London.

Matthew, HCG and Brian Harrison (eds.). 2004. *Oxford Dictionary of National Biography*. Oxford: Oxford University Press.

Medical Directory, The. 1927. London: Informa Healthcare.

Morgan, Janet. 1984. *Agatha Christie – A Biography*. London: Collins.

Perelberg, Rosine Josef (ed.). 2004. *Dreaming and Thinking*. London and New York: Karnak.

Robyns, Gwen. 1978. *The Mystery of Agatha Christie*. New York: Doubleday.

Semple, David, Roger Smyth, Jonathan Burns, Rajan Darjee and Andrew McIntosh. 2005. *Oxford Handbook of Psychiatry*: Oxford University Press.

Times, The. London.

Toye, Randal (compiler). 1980. *The Agatha Christie Who's Who*. Canada: Heron Books.

Westmacott, Mary. 1934. *Unfinished Portrait*. London: Collins.`

Wynne, Nancy Blue. 1976. *An Agatha Christie Chronology*. New York: Ace Books.

Television Documentaries

Flight, Collette (producer). 2004. *Agatha Christie: A Life in Pictures.* BBC. C. Wall to Wall Media. Described as 'A story based on documented accounts of the actual words of Agatha Christie'.

Warwick, Ben (writer and producer). 2005. *The Agatha Christie Code.* 3DD Productions.

Index

Forthcoming from Tempus:

Vanessa Bell by Frances Spalding
November 2006, ISBN 07524 4033 0
'Vanessa Bell emerges from Frances Spalding's sensitive and scholarly biography as an unexpectedly formidable figure, just as interesting, if not more so, than her sister.' *The Times*
'A courageously independent book...Vanessa, even more than Virginia, was Bloomsbury's hub... Excellent.' *The Guardian*
'An excellent biography: it could hardly be bettered... ' *John Russell, TLS*

Enid Blyton: The Biography by Barbara Stoney
November 2006 ISBN 07524 4030 6
'Admirably fair... the issues are faced and discussed with honesty and tact' *Daily Telegraph*
'This biography finds exactly the right tone. [Barbara Stoney] unravels the story with a directness that does not flinch from observation or blunder into tactlessness.' *Sunday Times*

A.A. Milne: His Life by Ann Thwaite
November 2006 ISBN 07524 4085 3
'Compelling, meticulous and very sensitive. I absolutely loved it.' *Andrew Motion*
'[Thwaite] has a Coleridgean gift for getting into the feel of her subject – the man, the age, the style.' *London Review of Books*
WINNER OF THE WHITBREAD BIOGRAPHY OF THE YEAR PRIZE

Dr James Barry: The Secret Life of Victorian England's Most Eminent Surgeon by Rachel Holmes
January 2007 ISBN 07524 4139 6
'A vivid and intelligent biography' *The Observer*
'Meticulously researched and fantastically discursive' *The Independent Magazine*
'Thrillingly romantic... paints an often gruesome picture of Victorian sexuality' *Daily Express*
'A wonderful read.' *Amanda Foreman, bestselling author of* Georgiana: Duchess of Devonshire

That Singular Person called Lear: The Extraordinary Life of the Author of the Owl and the Pussycat by Susan Chitty
February 2007 ISBN 07524 4137 X
'Deliciously amusing' *The Literary Review*
'A thorough and fascinating biography' *The Sunday Telegraph*
'An amusing biography' *The Independent*

Frances Hodgson Burnett: The Author of the Secret Garden by Ann Thwaite
February 2007 ISBN 07524 4138 8
'A fascinating and valuable book' *The Sunday Times*
'A glittering, lively story.' *The Observer*
'A model biography' *Daily Telegraph*

Elizabeth Robins by Angela V. John
March 2007 ISBN 07524 4028 4
'A sympathetic portrait based on meticulous scholarship' *Judith P. Zinsser, Miami University*
'A detailed, authoritative study of a remarkable woman.' *Norma Clarke*

Edmund Gosse: A Literary Landscape by Ann Thwaite
March 2007 ISBN 07524 4136 1
'Consistently absorbing and entertaining... It is a book which ought to appeal to anyone interested in the literary life of the period.' *The Observer*
'Magnificent... It is one of the finest literary biographies of all time.' *John Carey, The Sunday Times*
'Extremely enjoyable' *Daily Telegraph*